MW00614791

learning from the curse: Sembene's Xala

written by Richard Fardon
drawn by Sènga la Rouge

First published in the United Kingdom in 2017 by
C. Hurst & Co. (Publishers) Ltd.,
41 Great Russell Street, London, WC1B 3PL

Distributed in the United States, Canada and
Latin America by Oxford University Press,
198 Madison Avenue, New York, NY 10016,
United States of America.

A Cataloguing-in-Publication data record for this
book is available from the British Library.

9781849046954 hardback

This book is printed using paper from registered
sustainable and managed sources.

www.hurstpublishers.com

Graphic design: © Agnès Boulmer

learning from the curse: Sembene's Xala

written by Richard Fardon
drawn by Sènga la Rouge

contents

main characters

The Chamber of Commerce and its associates

Le Président – unnamed

Kebe, Le Député – elected by *'le peuple'* (film only)

Le Ministre – unnamed representative of *'le gouvernement'* (film only)

Members of the Board – **Cheikh Ba**, **Laye**, **Diagne** (those named in the book); **'Monsieur' Thieli** – a pickpocket who replaces El Hadji on the Board (film only)

Dupont-Durand – French adviser to the President of the Chamber

Two other European advisers (*tubabs*) – one acts as head of security (probably called Math, short for Mathieu), the other apparently as a financial intermediary (both in the film only)

The extended Bèye family and its staff

El Hadji Abdou Kader Bèye – the story's protagonist and head of the household

Adja Awa Astou (née Renée) – El Hadji's first wife; **'Papa Jean'** – her father, a third-generation Roman Catholic, he is *Maam* or grandfather to Rama (in the book version only); **Rama** – their daughter and oldest child; **'Mactar'** – the 'oldest son' of this marriage; **Pathé** – Rama's boyfriend (book version only)

Oumi N'Doye – El Hadji's second wife; **Mariem** – their teenage daughter; **'Mactar'** – the 'oldest son' of this marriage

N'Goné – El Hadji's nineteen-year-old third wife; *le vieux* (old) **Babacar** – her father (book only); **Mam Fatou** – her mother; **Yay Bineta** the *Badiène*[1] – Babacar's sister and N'Goné's father's sister or 'paternal aunt'; an unnamed **homme-femme** (man-woman) who is apparently Mam Fatou's retainer and – wedding reception *maître de cérémonie* (film only)

'Gorgui' Bèye – 'Old' Bèye, the clansman whose land El Hadji alienated

Modu – El Hadji's chauffeur of *la Mercédès*

Alassane – hyphenated *chauffeur-domestique*, driver-domestic servant of the family minibus (book only)

Madame Diouf – hyphenated *secrétaire-vendeuse*, secretary-saleswoman

Ahmed Tall – trading partner of Mauritanian origin

Others (some of them at least)

Serigne Mada, *Face-katt* (healer) – Modu's marabout

Seet-Katt (soothsayer) – unnamed in book, President's marabout in film, similar to Babacar's marabout in the book.

Unnamed: businessman (at wedding reception) (film only), banker at BCIAO (during denouement); *Kaddu* (Wolof-language newspaper) vendor; car washer (film only)

---

1. Bàjjan *is the transcription of the kinship term for father's sister in Jean-Léopold Diouf's* Wolof-French Dictionary.

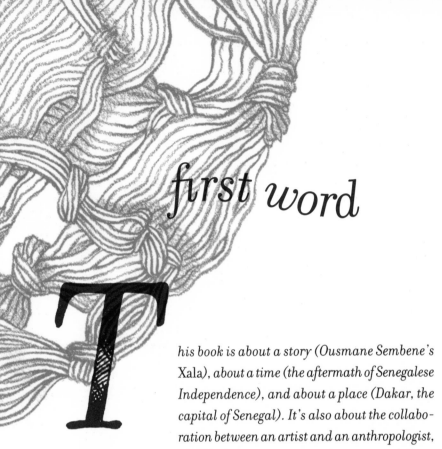

first word

T his book is about a story (Ousmane Sembene's Xala), about a time (the aftermath of Senegalese Independence), and about a place (Dakar, the capital of Senegal). It's also about the collaboration between an artist and an anthropologist, who have reacted in their different mediums to the story, time and place, and to what the other made of them.

The anthropologist, or from now on 'I', saw the Senegalese director Ousmane Sembene's film of Xala or 'The curse of impotence' for the first time in the late 1980s after I left a disciplinary teaching position in social anthropology to take up one that carried specific responsibility for West Africa at the School of Oriental and African Studies (SOAS) in the University of London. This was more than a decade after the film's original cinema release in 1974, which in turn had occurred a couple *of years before my first and longest West African residence (in Nigeria rather than Senegal). The facts of Xala being a film made just before I lived in West Africa, and my seeing it first when I was becoming a specialist teacher about that region, make those two formative times come freshly to mind each time I watch it.*

... and I have seen the film often. Most years when teaching the anthropology of West Africa, I have shown students some or all of Xala. I have worked my way through the only source I could find initially – a VHS cassette copied from a revelatory showing of a series of African films on television – via a proprietary cassette issued for the Africa95 festival in London (the cowry logo on its case recalling involvement in that event), and on to DVDs released in the USA and in France. Nowadays the film can also be found on YouTube. So, over time, Xala has become more tangled with my working life than any other film I can think of.

The screenplay of Xala was 'inspired', the verb used in the film credits, by Sembene's novella published in 1973 under the same title. Initially, I had intended to write only about the film, thinking that this later cinematic treatment supplanted the earlier text. But matters were less linear than this, as I soon realized: the novella was itself based on a screenplay, or at least film treatment, written while Sembene sought the financial backing to put the film into production. Moreover, Sembene often claimed to prefer his writing to his films, while conceding they reached different audiences: a film was accessible to a wider African audience than a book written in French. So, even if the film was made after the book had been written, at least for Sembene this did not grant it a finality the text lacked. Book and film were best treated even-handedly.

When I eventually set to work on my intention to write Sembene this posthumous note of appreciation, I returned to the film, viewing it several more times, and also reread the novella in its French original. Despite my familiarity with the story, this proved revelatory. I had thought the text lacked the ironies of the film, but this was true only of its English translation, which carried the plotline effectively but lost some cultural resonances of a Senegalese setting written about in French, as well as of Sembene's playful tone of voice. While film and novella share a central plot, they differ in their details without becoming incompatible for that. Some differences may be practical responses to the different mediums: for instance, most of a plot that unfolds over more than four months for the reader has been condensed into a few days for the screen viewer. But the major differences are of perspective, which is why jumping to the conclusion that the slightly later film supplanted the written version of the story proved so wrong. In scholarly parlance, the relation was better described as 'iterative', since screenplay and novella were successively revised versions of one another. The revisions did not end there, because Sembene's preoccupation with types of character and situation outlived the completion of Xala as both book and film. The novel Le dernier de l'empire (The Last of Empire), *set in a fictionalized Senegalese state that feels like that of Xala, was not published until 1981, but the dates of its composition run on from the release of Xala the film. A quarter century after Xala, Sembene's last but one completed film,* Faat Kine, *celebrated the life of a strong-willed business woman who fulfilled her ambitions despite the appalling behaviour of her father and lovers. The preoccupations of* Xala *remained the abiding concerns of Sembene's contemporary art.*

The novella of Xala *concerns the extended drama of an extended family, its entourage, and milieu, exploring the motives (mostly ignoble) of its main characters. There is an important political background to the story, without which the events lose much of their wider impact, but this context is political in the broad sense of the word. It has a number of axes (and axes to grind): authenticity and tradition against 'civilisation' and modernity; African against 'tubab' (or European, particularly French) values; generational changes and conflicts; the clashing needs of men and women, and of older and younger women, and the place of sexual politics in these; the growing gulf between rich and poor, even within extended families. Characters are given backstories, and inner musings to add psychological depth to these biographies. Much of this family drama, along with several of the significant family characters, disappears, or is diminished, in the film. By contrast, the film treats the personalities of the novella like political ciphers, or like personae whose attributes are attached to them materially and externally in the shapes of clothing, personal accoutrements, cars, houses, furniture, and names and phrases spoken so often they come to feel like solid attributes. Other personalities are added and aspects of the plot reshuffled to recentre the story as a political satire and a tragi-comedy (with abrupt switches between those two moods). While the broader political contexts remain evident (men and women, young and old, modernity* and authenticity, rich and indigent), a narrower politics that is more specifically Senegalese becomes prominent which most of the newly introduced characters are designed to exemplify. So, the film makes us look at what are for the most part the same events differently thanks to the ways they have been framed. Contrary to my first impression, the filmed story doesn't replace the textual story but supplements and only in some minor respects alters it.

Treating these two versions anthropologically, as cultural products, should have involved my contextualizing both rather than evaluating one as a more or less authentic expression of an authorial intention than the other. If I asked students to suspend disbelief in Sembene's story and characters and treat them as they might episodes and actors in an ethnographer's description, then I ought to follow this thought consistently myself. There is nothing odd in the ethnographic record about there being a pair of descriptions of the same social circumstances: one more curious about family, kinship and the networks of connections between people, the other covering much of the same ground from a narrower political viewpoint. Anthropologists have often written complementary accounts of kinship and politics (whether in the same or different books), and their readers have asked themselves whether the two perspectives fitted together without obvious contradictions. To my mind, the two versions of Xala *can be treated similarly, as largely complementary ethnographies of an imagined social network in Senegal, or more narrowly its capital Dakar, in the aftermath of formal Independence from France in 1960. They do not have to be read this way, and this reading does not preclude any other, but as a 'realist project', consistent with Sembene's Marxism, or even a 'neo-realist project', indebted to Italian post-war cinema, Xala — in both its versions — lends itself to such a reading.*

Quite how readily the versions spoke to one another became more obvious on two brief visits to Senegal while writing this account. I am no kind of expert on, let alone ethnographer of, Senegal. That would take years of intellectual investment in reading, language learning and patient residence. But to my anthropologist's sensibility some first-hand experience is qualitatively different from none at all, however short of real familiarity it falls. In early 2013 the Senegalese newspapers were filled with coverage of the fall from grace of their previous President, Abdoulaye Wade, and the allegations of corruption made against his family — notably his son Karim, ironized as the 'Minister of Heaven and Earth' on account of the range of his portfolios — for having others act as front men, or more evocatively in French 'prête-noms', *who 'lent' their names to cover his enrichment by directing public funds into private businesses via the works contracts they fronted. A return a year later found these issues apparently no closer to resolution. The degree to which family and politics merged was remarkable even by the standards of the places I was more familiar with — like Cameroon, Ghana, or Nigeria — that had larger casts of characters. Dakar, as a friend remarked, was really a village, and village gossip was widely shared. Dakar had been a much smaller village forty years earlier when Sembene conceived his characters and set their lives in motion at a time when other political and family destinies were even more closely entwined, notably those of Léopold Sédar Senghor, Sembene's sparring partner and President of Senegal for its first two post-Independence decades.*

So, this response is meant to repay in small measure the pleasures and insights I have gained from Xala as both book and film, and to explain why I have found it such a helpful toehold to offer students wanting to learn something about West African cultures and societies. This is not the account of a film buff or cinema theorist, or of a biographer of Ousmane Sembene, or of an expert on Senegal. In these three essential respects, I have leant on the work others. Instead, it is what this teacher of anthropology finds when he half-suspends disbelief in the characters and events of a fictionalized narrative and asks others to join him in this. As anthropologists have learnt in recent decades, interpretation of different genres of locally-grounded writings can pose similar challenges: both ethnographic accounts and socially aware fictions are based on the selective and artful re-presentation of actors and events. They may not be the same, but we can still bring some of the same techniques and curiosities to reading them.

If this account was to take both book and film as its subject, what then to do about illustration? The English translation of the novella Xala reproduced full-page stills from the film at paperback text quality, as murky as the smudged images of 1970s newspapers that might line old sock drawers. They detract both from the text, because the film images do not entirely fit that narrative (even in the physical description of some characters and scenes), and from the film, which has a slightly washed-out palette, similar to my surviving 35mm colour slides of the same period, but still imparts real vibrancy by shading the story in light and dark and in contrasting colours. So much of Xala is sensual and visual that entirely doing without images seemed as wrong as borrowing film frames.

How to escape from an impasse where illustration felt necessary but film stills were inadequate? I discussed the dilemma with the artist Sènga la Rouge whose illustrated travelogues had enchanted me. Would it be possible, we pondered, to produce images and design that, by not being illustrations, bore an exploratory relationship to their sources that was similar to my text? In their different ways, drawing and writing would respond to Xala in both of its realizations, and to each other, and — why not? — to the briefly experienced actuality of the country of Senegal forty years on from the main events of the story. So this is where we find ourselves, as I draft this first word, in the shaded courtyard of a hotel close to the settings of the drama of Xala at the end of a short visit to Senegal, seeking a textured response to Sembene's creation.

Only in the opening and closing scenes (the 'overture' and the 'denouement') do we follow the order of the plot. It is important to do so there to grasp the narrative and to appreciate its structure and its particular use of images of pollution and sexuality. What happens in the overture is reversed in the denouement, even to the extent of revisiting the locales of the scenes in reverse order. This possibility of symmetrical and opposite doing and undoing, tying and untying, is foreshadowed verbally more than once: 'what one hand does, another can undo', or 'what one plants another can uproot'. Moreover, the movement of the narrative from beginning to end takes us from aspirations to modernity and civilization, until the moment in the life of our main protagonist when his ascent towards these values is overwhelmed by everything — peasantry, poverty, rubbish — he has sought to transcend. The fall from grace of both the story's hero and his society means that the emotional tone of Xala, which has veered between comedy and tragedy, comes to rest on the tragic.

Dakar, April 2013 and April 2014

overture

overture: from the French ouverture, *the opening to an extended work, often in a distinct genre.*

ntroduce the story with the film, because its opening scenes are implied only in general terms by what later parts of the book tell us. These sequences of *Xala*, up to and including the bright-red credits rolling, are a favourite dozen minutes in African cinema (at least what I have seen of it, and I've seen more than a bit) and would be high up a list (if I had one) of my all-time favourite film sequences. Themes and characters are set in motion with absolute economy by a film maker not always

noted for compression (even in this film). This opening (and the closing that reverses it) need to be summarized closely for our later thematic discussion to make sense. If *Xala* was an opera, then this would be its particularly ingenious overture, foreshadowing the work's mood and events. Without giving the plot away, it supplements and puts it – and us – into a context.

[Insistent drumming]: from a low camera position, we pan in extreme close-up from a perspiring face, to a string of beads worn over a bright red t-shirt, to a blur of hands that resolves into a drum-skin pulsing from stick and palm; the camera draws back to reveal a four-man ensemble of drummers, and two dancers, a woman and a man in costumes decorated with cowry shells that shine in the sun and proclaim 'tradition'. It's a celebration, but of what?

Their backs to a rejoicing crowd – amongst whom the camera has taken us, to make us onlookers with this throng – a group of eight men in baggy trousers, coloured, loose smocks, a cap here, a straw hat there, shod in sandals – apparently modest, if new, local everyday dress rather than the self-consciously traditional garb of the dancers – energetically bound up a steep flight of stone steps into an imposing building of European neo-classical style. They are the cause of the jubilation. [At the appearance of the figures, the soundtrack superimposes a speech over what we understand to be the ambient sounds of drums and shouting: '*Monsieur le Ministre, Monsieur le Député, Honorables Collègues* .... Never before has an African occupied the Presidency of our Chamber (in full, *Chambre de Commerce*, as the camera's slow pan of the inscription above the building's entrance tells us), we must take back what is ours and reverts to us by right; we must control our industry, business and culture ... and take in hand our *destiny* ...'] By now the small party has entered a meeting room inside the Chamber of Commerce, where three *tubabs*, or Europeans, are seated to one side of the main table; behind them is an elaborate panel with an outline image of the *Presqu'île de Cap Vert*, the peninsula which has Dakar at its tip, with the Ile de Gorée a very short distance out to sea. The Europeans wear different shades of tinted sunglasses, with white shirts under dark blazers or suits, a style of dress that means business. The central figure is striking: a full drooping moustache, sideburns, longish hair (combed over both a balding pate and his shirt collar), pocket handker-chief foppishly drooping from the breast pocket of a double-breasted suit, chunky metal-link man-bracelet – apogee of a certain 1970s style. We shall learn later that he is Dupont-Durand, an everyman French name. The men flanking him are neater in appearance, more clipped in 1960s-style tonsorially: to his right, Dupont-Durand's companion, Math, wears intimidatingly dark sunglasses given that we are indoors, which immediately lend him a sinister impression. The companion to his left looks more like an accountant. Together they will evoke politics, force and finance. [We still hear the disembodied speech, and the drumming from outside.] On the word 'destiny', the group of intruders strips the Chamber of most of its ornaments and equipment, including a bust of Marianne standing, incongruously alongside a pair of military boots, on a red pedestal with blue background against the white wall. Only the diminutive man at their head remains to fix the three Europeans with a pantomime stare of resolution. He has placed a rectangular par-cel wrapped in brown paper on the table. Meanwhile, his companions have removed the offending objects: Marianne, the gleaming, marmoreal woman of the people in her Phrygian cap is placed on the steps, where she is joined by an equally blanched, but elaborately coiffured, bust of the regal Marie Antoinette. A couple of kepis (French military peaked caps), a khaki slouch hat, and two pairs of highly polished army boots are more or less chucked after them. There is a rapid juxtaposing cut from the still, white marble portraits of the French women (recall that the Greek-garbed Marianne in the guise of liberty – familiar to generations from French banknotes and stamps – is most famously represented bare-breasted by Delacroix's 1830 *La liberté guidant le peuple*) to the bouncing breasts of a vigorously dancing Senegalese woman in the crowd. [The drumming and celebration continue on the soundtrack, so does the speech. 'Before our people, we must show that we are as capable as other people in the world ...']

The group re-enters the Chamber to join their leader. ['We are businessmen (*hommes d'affaires* – the first occurrence of a phrase that will recur with building significance and irony) and must take control, even of the banks ...'] The (Chaplinesque) leader continues to fix the Europeans with a stare, pointing at them one by one, and gesturing them to leave, which they do calmly, almost wearily, after capping their pens, and arranging the papers in front of them on the table [the action is as broad as silent film, the voiceover continues, 'our Independence is complete; today is a historic day ..']. On the steps, the three Europeans cradle the busts and collect the boots and hats [still the crowd cheers, the drummers play, and the disembodied voice continues '... it is a victory, a victory of our people; the sons of the people lead the people in the interest of the people']. Another shot of drumming, the group of Africans framed by the portico of the Chamber of Commerce raise their arms in triumph towards the crowd below to embrace their acclamation. More drums and horns, and they disappear back into the Chamber of Commerce. (The film has been running just two and a half minutes.)

Re-entry from screen left [ominously the drumming has ceased]: a column of eight African troops in generic khaki uniforms, with berets, Sam Browne belts, and polished boots under the command of the sharp and sinister European who wears dark glasses (as does the soldier at the head of the column). (We shall learn later that these are the state security, called here Cerbères, like the violent stewards/bouncers the French idiom analogizes to Cerberus, hellhound guardian of the door to the Greek god Hades' underworld.) They begin to push back the crowd. (Has time passed? It both has and hasn't.) A dance troupe is still present, and the crowd is composed largely of women still dressed in their finest. Dupont-Durand and the European who looked like an accountant, walk into the ample space cleared by force and mount the steps back into the building from which they were lately evicted; they carry seven attaché cases. [The camera lingers as the soles of their shoes crunch on the road, synching sound and picture to the slower rhythm of their pace. As they mount the steps, the off-screen orator proclaims, 'We opt for socialism, the only true socialism, the African socialist way, people's socialism. Our Independence is complete.']

The camera has re-entered the Chamber where we discover the sometime intruders in African dress have made themselves comfortable at the table around which they now sit in evening dress; even the ashtrays left by the Europeans remain in place. On the word 'Independence' the parcel wrapped in brown paper is torn open by the leader to reveal that he had brought along (while he still wore African dress) a portrait of himself, posed in the evening suit (or tuxedo) and bow-tie he now wears; he props this on the red-cloth covered plinth previously occupied by the portrait bust of Marianne and army boots. The members of the Chamber stand to applaud; a gesture acknowledged with a modest nod by the new President of the Chamber as he walks around the table to take the seat Dupont-Durand occupied previously. The two Europeans re-enter the Chamber [their shod footsteps loud on the floor]. They place an attaché case in front of each member of the Chamber of Commerce then station themselves behind the President, and before a framed political map of African nation states in Mercator projection that now hangs on the wall occupied by the inlaid panel depicting the Dakar peninsular, which has been crudely covered with brown paper held in place by drawing pins.[1] In silence, other than the sharp clicks of case locks being sprung, starting with the elected *Député* who is the only one of them in a white dinner jacket, we watch the members of the Chamber lift the case lids just sufficiently to see their contents. Each grins with quiet, complicit satisfaction. The contents are hidden to us, until we look into his attaché case from the viewpoint of the President of the Chamber of Commerce. This case, and presumably the others too, are chock-a-block with bundles of 5,000 CFA notes (each worth a

----

1. *The political map and tailored, formal suits are associated visually. The same framed map hangs on the wall of El Hadji's office behind him in a scene when he is confronted by his daughter Rama. The map behind her is of an unpartitioned Africa outlined in deep, bright colours that match her clothes.*

little less than $20 in the mid-1970s). The President looks at Dupont-Durand who bows with measured deference; the President nods; we cut briefly to his Presidential photograph, with its determined expression, propped on the red plinth, with a blue background (almost the same blue as the table covering), against a white wall (the previously French *tricolore* colour coding unchanged to the Senegalese green, yellow and red).

The President of the Chamber of Commerce rises and clears his throat to read a prepared speech [he opens with the honorifics we heard earlier, so we immediately recognize his as the voice of the disembodied orator; but now image and speech have synched into a cinematic present tense, 'Our revolutionary action was not in vain; our presence in the Chamber of Commerce and Industry has been sanctioned by a text from our illuminating guide and father of the nation.' Applause and bravoes. The speech has more in the same vein.] As the President closes his address he turns to the distinguished looking white-haired man seated to his right, who we learn is El Hadji Abdou Kader Bèye. El Hadji has just taken his third wife. ['Our modernity must not let us lose our Africanity!'. More vigorous assent, particularly from the *Député*.] El Hadji is formally passed '*la parole*' with French committee etiquette. He announces that the religious ceremony for his taking a third wife has just finished and he invites all present to join him for the wedding reception that night at which 'nothing will be lacking'. [More smiles and applause.] Using the handbell left on the table by the colonial regime, and flanked by the two Europeans, the President announces the meeting closed ('*La séance est levée*').

being all for modernity does not mean losing our africanity

A broad red carpet is unrolled cascadingly down the front steps, at the head of which the President appears rapt in conversation with the ever-attentive Dupont-Durand; he descends followed by the remainder of the meeting, all with attaché cases in hand, the European accountant bringing up the rear. The sinister European in dark glasses is vigilantly, even officiously, taking care of transport, the arrival of which is announced by sirens and uniformed motorcycle outriders. Dupont-Durand opens the rear door for the President of the Chamber to enter a large American Ford at the head of a small cavalcade of vehicles. Next along comes a shining black Mercedes with the squared headlamps of the then, 1970s, latest model. The head of security opens the door for the *Député* in the white dinner jacket to enter. The chauffeur stalls this vehicle as he leaves [someone cackles in the crowd; was this serendipity that Sembene let stand? Inability to command technology is a leitmotif as we shall discover]. A pale blue Mercedes with rounded headlamps, hence of slightly earlier vintage, is the third vehicle up for the Minister. The camera pulls back and we see the convoy of eight vehicles (mostly Mercedes, with a Citroen DS near the back) head off from the Chamber behind the outriders and up Dakar's central square, the Place de l'Indépendance, on a corner of which the Chamber of Commerce stands. Meanwhile across town in a carefully-tended, European-style garden, we find three mature women, looking their best in printed dresses with matching headscarves. One of them, a praise singer with the bank notes she has been 'dashed' pinned to her blouse, wears a wrapper on which are printed the faces of an African man and European woman, reminiscent of President Léopold Sédar Senghor and his French wife, Colette Hubert. The mother of El Hadji's third wife is showing the wedding gifts given by her daughter's new husband to the other two admiring women, one of whom we shall learn is Badiène, or father's sister, to the bride. She explains in Wolof [which we hear distinctly now for the first time] what they are: a television, the keys to a car [the friend ululates her approval of this], a jewel box full of gold .... Having also made its way around the Place de l'Indépendance, a second cavalcade [horns blaring] of more modest vehicles is converging on this place carrying the young bride in the most conventional of white western bridal gowns and veils; it includes a car carrier loaded with a small eggshell-blue Fiat (tied with white ribbons) to which we just saw the keys.

Roll red credits over the bustle of a modern city (which we shall realize is Dakar, the capital of Senegal, its skyline dominated by the minaret of the Grande Mosquée finished a decade earlier in 1964). We hear the voice of a griot singing music credited to Samba Diabara Samb, a *xalam*, or lute, player, to which Sembene himself wrote the Wolof lyrics, as we see the wedding processions passing through the outskirts of Dakar towards one of its prosperous suburbs. Against the roads and modern tower blocks, and the sounds and sights of traffic, a walking figure in a short white gown is foregrounded, the everyman of urban society; the camera regards him from the angle we might if we sat at curb level. This is someone's view, but whose?

We are about eleven minutes into the 123 minutes of the film.

The cinematic language of these opening scenes – cuts to shift our attention, telescoped temporal development, disjunctions and conjunctions between soundtrack and images – put what we might call – in homage to Dupont-Durand's comb-over, and borrowing the phrase for downsizing applied during recent, global financial travails – the neo-colonial 'haircut' before us with speed and irony. The film and novella treatments are at their most divergent here. In the film version, fine words about African Independence are the prelude to the businessmen taking ownership of 'the Chamber', from which the trio of Europeans are absent for just the time it takes the Africans to sit themselves in the same positions at table as their erstwhile colonial masters, who shuffle into deferential, but all-seeing, positions over the President's shoulder. More fine words about Africanity are uttered as the businessmen's everyday African dress (do we really believe they wore it other than to pander to the crowd?) is replaced by western evening wear, and Africanity is cited as one justification (there will be others) for a middle-aged man's 'duty' to take a third wife of his oldest daughter's age. Yet more fine words are spouted about a victory shared with the crowd, or masses, as police sirens wail at the head of an elite procession, so that state menace and the rulers' celebrations ascend together in pitch.

Two of the sharply-dressed Europeans have a relatively timeless appearance: the security man with dark glasses is a rigid, unsmiling figure fitting his line of work. Dupont-Durand's assistant in distributing attaché cases of money looks like the accountant, or at least penny counter, he may well be. But it was always Dupont-Durand who fascinated me. He could exist only in the early 1970s. The double-breasted suit and pocket handkerchief may have looked sharp to someone at the time, though I wonder whom, but the passage of epochs has indexed such appearance to the decade that style forgot. It's the hair that clinches the neo-colonial moment. Filling in the balding pate, removing the Zapata moustache and luxuriant sideburns, and cropping the flaps of hair tucked behind his ears and draped over his shirt collar, would turn this wannabe trendy character back into the colonial creature we should have understood him to be. He has not been mutated by the 1970s, which would involve a difference in the posture and overall clothed shape of the body and hair (in that difficult-to-define way that corporeal signature changes between fashion eras), but simply allowed the style he already had to become slightly unkempt. It's in the same unconvincing way (for those of us whose young adulthood occurred then) that some French actors (think of Jean-Paul Belmondo or Jean-Pierre Léaud) became slightly frayed and dishevelled, versions of their sharper, younger selves. If Senegal, on Sembene's analysis, gets a neo-colonial haircut, then Dupont-Durand is that haircut, and if this is, and it is, a seriously intended exposé of neo-colonialism, it's all done with a knowing, if not entirely amused, wink. The new bourgeoisie is ridiculous as well as corrupt.

More generally, the lucidity of this scene-setting overture depends on a set of visual statements made about bodily deportment, styles of dress, and material culture, both local and imported. Some of the imported culture is designed to make specific symbolic statements (like the portrait busts of Marianne and Marie Antoinette) but most of it carried wider cultural resonances through appropriation in a 1970s West African context, and not always the same significances it had in the place it came from: for instance, the attention paid to the differentiation of models of the Mercedes (always Mercedes, or some other marque, and never just cars) that became in Nigeria the quintessential marker of the rich, necessarily 'corrupt' patron-politician. My own – kind and supportive – Chamba sponsor and 'elder brother', a First Republic politician adopting a low profile in his home town during the military regime (a relatively benevolent regime by later standards I discovered only in retrospect) had a light blue Mercedes saloon that was used to move even the shortest distance (like that between his bungalow and the palace at which he was the Wakili – Prime Minister – all of 500 yards away). I didn't remark this then as an ethnographic fact worth recording, as I now would. When, a quarter of a century later, I drove a thirsty, rusting Mercedes of similar vintage around London (until I could no longer afford the fuel for it), my West Africanist work colleague remarked with good humour that I resembled a Nigerian Second Republic politician fallen on hard times. Which is what a distressed Mercedes had come to signify by then. Incidentally, since Sembene's sensitivity to commodities has this effect on viewers, El Hadji's white Mercedes limousine looks like a 200 series *Neue Klasse* (the 'New Class', introduced in 1968) saloon to me (perhaps a 280S): a statement of wealth and standing. By report, the film of *Xala* briefly made driving a Mercedes in Dakar an embarrassment. The age of the luxury limousine was overtaken by an age of the SUV and 4x4, in which the Pajero, the must-have transport of the NGOs, took the palm. The car parks of the Dakarois elite are now full of vaguely military looking vehicles, Land Cruisers with darkened windscreens. What the Mercedes was to a reception room, a display meant to attract admiring attention, the SUV has become to a gated compound, exclusion made manifest.

We shall need to come back to the metonymic, part-standing-for-whole, statues of boots, portrait busts, sunglasses, attaché cases, business suits and so forth later, but enough for now about the set-up that is the film's overture and establishes the tone of the tragi-comic opera to follow. What of the book?

The three *tubabs*, specifically Frenchmen, do not appear in the book narrative at all, and while we are told that the members of what they prefer to abbreviate, from 'megalomania', to 'the Chamber' were youthful firebrands in the independence struggle, the entire scene of their assumption of power is witnessed only in the film. The novel begins with the President's speech that is addressed not to the masses but to the members of the Chamber, and his invitation to their 'brother' (rather than colleague) to address those assembled about his third marriage, the religious elements of the ceremony for which were taking place even as they gathered. El Hadji Abdou Kader Bèye is clearly self-satisfied and announces that in taking a third wife he has become what among '*la populace*' is called a '*capitaine*', the biggest of the big fish at the top of the feeding chain, with its distinctive dorsal fins like sails.[2] We learn that he has made his money in cahoots with Lebanese and Syrian businessmen (an outsider slot occupied in the film by the northern, Mauritanian, trader, Ahmed Fall), in part as a *prête-nom* (someone who 'lends his name' to front business transactions). The idiom is significant given the importance of naming to Senegalese notions of status and honour. To sum him up, following Sembene, in terms none of which need translation: '*Formation bourgeoise européenne, éducation féodale africaine*'. 'Like his peers, he knew how to make best use of these two poles. The fusion was not complete.' ('*Il savait, comme ses pairs, se servir adroitement de ses deux pôles. La fusion n'était pas complète.*') He had 'played the game' ('*Il joua le jeu*'). Or, as another character infers, he is that classificatory anomaly, an African *tubab*: black-skinned with a white mask as Sembene would have known Frantz Fanon put it.

Xala the novella introduces the plot on a scale that is more intimate, biographical and private than the film: kinship, pseudo-kinship, upbringing and identity, and eating. These will provide just as much of a roller coaster ride as the more public scale of the film, but with different attention to detail. Whereas the film's characters

----

2. *The English translation is unhelpful in several respects for this scene. 'Brother' becomes 'colleague', hence missing the claim to elite kinship, and 'un capitaine' seems to be interpreted as a military rank and not a fish, which would make a later reference to 'harpooning' in the text incomprehensible were it not (mis)translated as 'caught out'. The snappy tone of 'Il joua le jeu' is flattened by the English translation, 'he played his various roles well'. It would be tedious to go on, but readers of the English text need to be aware that the plotline is accurate but the tone a bit tin-eared.*

are initially collections of attributes, the cast of the novel are personalities from the outset. Even without these differences, the film would be more provocative. Recall that the panel of the Dakar peninsular had been covered in makeshift fashion with a map of Africa. Sembene is evidently analogizing 'the Chamber' to the Senegalese state, and its bow-tied President both to Léopold Sédar Senghor, first President of independent Senegal, and to Charlie Chaplin (not coincidentally 'The Great Dictator'), whom Sembene particularly admired.[3] The opening scenes were shot at the real Chamber of Commerce, a colonial building of 1926 on a corner of the Place de l'Indépendance, Dakar's most significant public ceremonial space. Before Independence this had been the Place Protêt, named after the Captain who moved France's military presence onshore there from the Ile de Gorée in the mid-nineteenth century. The monument for the fallen stood there, and it was there that Independence was declared. By having his story begin where it did, Sembene could not have given viewers familiar with Dakar a clearer indication of what it was to be about as a political allegory: the legacy of colonialism, and the appearance and reality of Independence.

A tricky question now: should we get the plot out of the way, or leave the *dénouement*, appropriately a literal unknotting, to the final pages? I think you need to know, if you don't know it already, the outline of what happens, though I'll hold back on El Hadji's sticky end (if you don't yet know that too).

----

3. *Later we see that a poster of Charlie Chaplin faces one for Sembene's previous film,* Le Mandat, *on the bedroom walls of El Hadji's daughter.*

The *xala* of the title is Wolof for the affliction of impotence, presumed to have been sprung on account of the resentment of another. El Hadji finds he is suffering from *xala* when he tries to consummate his third marriage and cannot. In the novel, Sembene uses the phrase for a medieval French magical practice, *nouer l'aiguillette*, or knotting the cord of the cod-piece. Who caused this, and how to fix, or unknot, it are the main concerns of the story. Suspicion falls upon his two wives, particularly the second of them, strongly contrasted characters as we shall see, but the real agent of his misfortune has been present virtually throughout in the person of a beggar, or in the film the leader of a group of beggars, who turns out to be a clansman cheated of land sold by El Hadji to get his start in business. Only by acknowledging his family, land and place of origin can El Hadji be restored his manhood. In these most pared-down terms, *Xala* the film/novella is about the impotence of the new Senegalese middle class, 'who had given themselves the right to the pompous title "businessmen" (*hommes d'affaires*) but were no more than intermediaries, a new kind of salesman (*commis*)'. *Xala* and its cumulative consequences trigger the worst nightmare of the new African bourgeoisie, a complete unravelling of every step they had taken – whether material or cultural – on the road to *civilisation* and personal promotion.

With the most basic plot elements outlined, we can flesh out the plotlines thematically.

patriarchy unplugged

*polygyny: the marriage of a man
to more than one woman.*

ala is a drama both about political economy, in a broad sense, and about the affairs of the family, including marriage and sex, and the spaces in which these are played out. The affairs of the family and the state become impossible to distinguish, as they tend to be in contemporary Senegalese politics. For a marxist, like Sembene, economy and family are both about processes of reproduction, and the relations of inequality which arise through these. The book and film accentuate these interests differently: the book offers more detail from the domestic perspective and the film from the context of an implied national state politics. While the main cast of characters is the same in both versions, there are changes of personnel around the edges of them, both in terms of their numbers, and in terms of what we learn about them and how they are introduced to us.

It is El Hadji's initial circulation between his various residences en route to his wedding reception that provides the opportunity for Sembene to tell us about his complicated, polygynous, family life and, particularly in the book, about the back stories of his various arrangements. Book and film correspond quite closely in their openings in this respect, as they will when reversing the opening sequence of events to reach their conclusion.

We first learned of El Hadji's third marriage in the Chamber of Commerce, which is appropriate given the commodity character of the young bride that Sembene will insist upon. El Hadji's claim in the film to have acted out of duty (*devoir*) in making this marriage rings hollow from the outset. Leaving the Chamber, El Hadji cannot continue with the cavalcade of luxury cars heading towards the wedding reception because he has to pick up his first two wives from the villas in desirable residential quarters of Dakar outside the old city centre where he has installed them with his children. We are taken initially to the house of Adja, his first wife (or Awa). She lives in a modern home decorated in African-inflected style with her six children, two of whom are made representative of the rest. The oldest daughter, Rama, continues an abandoned possibility of her father's trajectory, since she is a political radical and

Wolof language activist, as well as a self-possessed young woman in control of her body, her appearance and her life. Serious-minded but also sensual, to judge by the relationship with Pathé, her doctor and psychiatrist boyfriend, that is developed in the book (but absent from the film), Rama presents one possibility of synthesis between African identity and western technologies. In the book she has the same model of Fiat coupé that El Hadji gives his third wife as a wedding present, with the significant difference that she actually drives it around, even at excessive speed; in the film this transport is reduced to a smaller, contrastive, unit of mobility, a mobylette (motor-cycle with pedals) on which she scoots herself around town and notably to Dakar's university. Rama wears her hair in practical styles, with or without short plaits, and typically dresses in brightly coloured blouses in 'African' patterns over trousers. If she is serious-minded, it is in a good sense, supportive of her mother and the only person in El Hadji's immediate entourage willing to be critical of him openly for his taking a third wife on the grounds of tradition while he inconsistently insists on the exclusive use of French language and French commodities (most obviously represented by bottled Evian water). Her father's slap across her face in response to her accusation is particularly shocking for occurring within this female domestic space and in the context of a dispute about standards of civilization. Rama's brother, 'Mactar' (an honorific for oldest brother) is little more than a cipher, but we learn from his only demand on his father, for school money, that he shares Rama's commitment to education.

El Hadji's first wife has been with him for twenty years and married him for love, contrary to the wishes of her Roman Catholic father, Papa Jean, who distrusted the young firebrand. Under her baptismal name of Renée, Adja Awa Astou was brought up on the Ile de Gorée, a very short distance offshore from Dakar. This was not then the world heritage site in the history of slavery and the tourist destination that it has become subsequently, but an enclave of Roman Catholics in a country that is predominantly (more than 90%) Muslim. Her father, who appears in the book but not film and is visited by his grand-daughter Rama on the island, remains unreconciled to his daughter's marriage, indeed his antipathy increased when she found herself made so soon into a co-wife. He recalls a period when the Christian community attended the great holidays in the lovely church of Saint Charles Borromée on the island dressed up in their best clothes. For these attitudes, he was labelled a neo-colonialist by the young El Hadji (or as he would have been then, plain Abdou Kader Bèye). Father and daughter became estranged once Jean's wife, Renée/Astou's mother, died.

Abdou Kader Bèye's ascent to wealth must have been as meteoric as the overture to the film suggests, since three years after his first marriage he took a second wife, Oumi N'Doye. As a consolation to Adja Awa Astou, we are told that she went on pilgrimage to Mecca, hence becoming Adja (pilgrim), and Awa (senior wife), at the same time. Increasingly devout, we infer as compensation (even over-compensation, since Sembene calls religion her drug) for the disappointment of the emotional trust she had placed in her husband, the book tells us (though the film does not show this) that she typically dressed all in white. She is a woman in her late thirties, more than a decade younger than her husband in his fifties, elegant and measured in her gestures usually occupied with white prayer beads (perhaps bought in Mecca) or the local chewing sticks that serve as toothbrushes. In western terms, she might be considered a 'younger' woman, but we are soon disabused of this conception in relation to El Hadji. Men and women have different life cycles. Should she leave her husband, she tells her daughter Rama in Wolof, in reaction to criticism of her 'patience' (*muñ*), a woman of her age could anticipate no better than to be a co-wife placed well down the pecking order in another polygynous household. At least she has the dignity of being Awa in El Hadji's extended household and, with consequences that we see later, the owner of her own villa.

Once Adja Awa has been installed alongside him in the back of the Mercedes, El Hadji, with his chauffeur Modu at the wheel wearing his best white uniform, heads off to pick up his second wife. Oumi N'Doye's villa is similar to Adja Awa's but differently furnished, as we begin to learn from the more ornate house name-plate the book describes before we have even entered. Oumi is a contrasting character to Adja Awa: extravert, sensuous, highly sexed, and besotted with things European, particularly French, she became her husband's favourite. Prayer beads and tooth sticks are not for this woman, who instead fiddles with or chews on her fashionable sunglasses. We first meet her as her long, manicured nails tease the wig with which she fusses; she is bare-shouldered in a little black cocktail dress and high heels. Thoroughly urban, Oumi subsists on a diet of fashion magazines and photo-romances which provide the stuff of her dreams; at home in a world of brand names and labels, we are told that her furniture carries the *griffe* 'made in France' (whether or not, we might infer, it was). Her five children contrast with Adja's in the same ways that she does. Like her mother, the daughter, Mariem dresses immodestly, by what we infer would be Adja's standards. The novel cites her mini-skirt. And, like her mother, Mariem is comfortable with overt sensuality and makes immediate physical contact with her father (by contrast, the first touch we witness between El Hadji and Adja's family is when he slaps Rama for calling polygynists liars). Mariem and her brother, as well as their mother, make insistent demands on him for money without specifying an educational purpose for it. We are invited to deduce that Oumi was the status symbol and erotic present the successful El Hadji made himself in his mid-thirties. We learn nothing about either her natal family or previous circumstances: Oumi is presented to us unanchored, as an individual in a European-style marital home, but also as a realist, who accepted her husband as a polygynist.

The tension between the co-wives is quickly apparent. Adja refuses to enter Oumi's villa, preferring to wait in the car below, but we learn that she at least has set foot there previously, whereas Oumi has never in her seventeen years of marriage visited the place her husband goes to live when he leaves her bed to fulfil the sleeping, eating and sexual schedule of his polygynous marriage. Unable to determine which of his wives will sit in the less prestigious front seat alongside the chauffeur, El Hadji is wedged between them on the back seat – Oumi draped possessively over his left shoulder, Adja independently upright to his right, attaché case behind them on the back ledge – as together they head off to a third villa he has had to acquire for his third wife. This is in one of the newer residential suburbs of the expanding city, and seems to have more spacious grounds from what we see of the wedding reception.

As Sembene remarks in his written treatment, polygynous husbands in the city are obliged to maintain separate premises for each of their wives at what, we can readily appreciate, must be considerable cost. Circulating between these places, in accordance with the *moomé* or *ayé* rota (as Sembene explains, the number of days spent with each wife), to fulfil their duties as husband (Oumi's demands we learn being considerably more strenuous than Adja's in this aspect of polygynous marriage) the men really have nowhere to call their own. El Hadji's office in the filmed version of the story looks rather better appointed than that described in the book: a corner of a warehouse, hedged in by a few filing cabinets, and with a couple of chairs picked up in a second-hand sale. Later in the story, needing a few hours of repose, El Hadji can find respite only in places run by expatriates: a Frenchman's restaurant, and a Syrian's hotel, which he also used on those occasions when he had the energy for extra-marital assignations with girlfriends. Homelessness is the price of urban polygyny.

45

Perhaps N'Goné, the third wife, is the kind of girl who might have been, or will become, a rich man's girlfriend. Although in the film she seems to represent the purity of the bride in white, the presence of a naked photograph of herself on the bedroom wall of her new villa strikes a discordant note. What is this image doing on the wall of a virgin bride, and who took it, since it looks a professional portrait? Even if banal, these seem legitimate questions to ask of a realist film. Is this simply a crude reference to commodification on Sembene's part? Part of the analogy consists in her almost entirely wordless role; she does speak once in the film, but then about her body to confirm to El Hadji that he cannot sleep with her because it is her period. Even that statement is uttered off-screen, so we never see N'Goné speak; an inarticulate shriek is the only other sound we hear from her. The book confirms what the film infers, that N'Goné's behaviour has been a source of constant concern to her family, and part of the reason that she has been married off to an older man. Even in the film she is told of her good fortune, because it is rare to be wed these days. The boys she hangs out with at the beginning of the novella's version of the story have to be discouraged to clear the way for the approach to El Hadji; and once she is divorced from El Hadji, Sembene as novelist lingers in his description of the tightly-trousered buttocks of the young man she takes up with. On her bridal night, even N'Goné's own mother is unsure of her virginity, and the services of a woman ready to kill a cockerel to provide the evidential blood stain are

put in hand.¹ Patience running out, her provocation of the impotent El Hadji by opening her legs wide is not written as if it was that of an unworldly girl. If N'Goné is a commodity, then Sembene suggests that the buyer should beware, in case he is being sold only the appearance of a good corresponding to his desires. Rama, expressing an antagonism that is absent from the cinema version, more bluntly describes to her own boyfriend the likelihood of her father's new wife being a virgin (*pucelle*) being as great as she being virginal herself (a likelihood of which he should have certain knowledge), while she previously described N'Goné to her mother as a slut (*salope*, 'whore' in the English translation).

Ironically, El Hadji the salesman is sold on N'Goné by a woman he has known for many years and who knows how to play him like the 'big fish' he is, at least in his own eyes. The woman with the title Badiène, N'Goné's father's sister, has the standing of a 'husband' to N'Goné's mother and wields equivalent authority. Consistent with this kinship reasoning, N'Goné is the Badiène's daughter, as well as her own father's. This woman – something of a grotesque in the book, at which the film also hints – has seen off two husbands and is suspected of causing their deaths, whether or not purposefully. Perhaps bad luck simply follows her, but no other man will take a risk on her, as she knows well. Her view of marriage is correspondingly unromantic, and she is keen to marry off the ill-educated and

----

1. *The English translation describes this killing as a 'sacrifice', but in reality it is a deception, and the French verb used, immoler, does not seem to warrant this gloss, particularly as the killing is to take place between N'Goné's thighs.*

irresponsible N'Goné to a wealthy man. El Hadji fits the bill well, and the Badiène understands perfectly how to work on his male vanity in its specifically Wolof form by luring him into a game of competitively allusive, verbal sparring.

The more El Hadji gets to know N'Goné, the more he finds her vacuous and tedious. In the film as well as in the book, she is reduced not just to a body which is the object of possessive desire, but to the prey about to be penetrated by the hunting bird El Hadji. This is ironic, since El Hadji is himself prey for the Badiène. Outwardly, N'Goné is the icon of the bride as she appears in the twin model figures of the bride and groom atop the six-tiered wedding cake, an icon that Oumi, no longer the youngest wife, lifts between two fingers with such quizzical disdain, to tug at the bride's veil.[2] Once she removes her veil and wedding gown, N'Goné's wedding costume hangs from a dress maker's mannequin[3] in her bedroom, mocking El Hadji there, until it is transported at the film's culmination to the home of his first wife, as the only trace that remains of this failed late effort to signal his 'big-fish' status. The mannequin is itself an Afro-European fusion, composed of a conventional dummy's body surmounted with a basketry wig-stand and a black wig (not, in fact, worn by the bride when we see her).

----

2. *Akin Adesokan makes a point of Oumi snapping the head off the bridal figure, but this does not happen in any cut of the film I have seen. She only tugs at its headdress.*
3. *Both words of the English translation as 'tailor's dummy' miss the gendered, erotic point here. Dressmakers' stalls in Dakar markets display mannequins in an abundance that seems designed as much to make discreet play on the female form to be clothed as to serve the practical purposes of displaying or fitting costumes.*

The relationship dynamics between *Xala*'s female characters are rebalanced to some degree between book and film, notably by downplaying the tensions between N'Goné's mother and her husband's sister (the Badiène), and between Rama and N'Goné. The male characters are more radically reshaped in the move from a kinship-focused to a politically-slanted account. Rama's doctor boyfriend disappears entirely from the film, along with a sub-plot that has El Hadji unsuccessfully seeking western as well as African cures for his condition of impotence. Papa Jean, the father of El Hadji's first wife Adja who recalls the halcyon days of the importance of the Catholic community on the Ile de Gorée, disappears too, as does the Ile de Gorée as a location. N'Goné's father, *le vieux* or 'old' Babacar, a hen-pecked man under the thumb of his wife, also goes. So does, Alassane, the hyphenated family driver-cum-domestic servant who ferries around the children from El Hadji's two marriages together in the same small bus.

The new and strengthened male figures tend not to be kin but political actors in narrow and broad senses. The number of marabouts El Hadji consults at great expense is drastically reduced between text and film, but the two who remain are sharply contrasted, as we shall see shortly. The cast of political actors is notably augmented by the three European neo-colonialists, representing politics, force and finance, whom we met in the film's opening, and by an initially nameless pickpocket who takes El Hadji's seat in the Chamber towards the film's conclusion. Businessmen and a banker feature in both versions without being strongly characterized, but the film adds a meeting between a businessman and the *Député* during the wedding reception in order specifically to introduce an instance of graft in the award of contracts and permissions. It cannot be accidental that the project discussed concerns tourism, which in the absence of internal tourism is a service provided only to foreigners, also to be cited by the President as one of the grounds for the eviction of beggars from the city.

Despite being titled after a sexual dysfunction, neither the film nor the book of *Xala* shows much interest in observing or describing sexual encounters. As Sembene remarked laconically in interview, we don't need to be shown sex because we all know what is involved.[4] His interest is drawn more to the politics of gendered roles, and the relations between men and women, of which sex is only a part. The instances of sexual attraction in the film are few: there is mildly salacious banter with complicit smiles between Ahmed Fall, the trader, and Madame Diouf, the secretary-saleswoman, at El Hadji's warehouse-cum-office, which gives us the impression that this has been a long-running gag, or joking relationship, between them; and there is Oumi's considerable enthusiasm on El Hadji's showing up at her villa when N'Goné's period frustrates his bid to consummate his third marriage; but that is about the sum of erotic interest in sexual relations. Even El Hadji's sexual interest in his young bride is described as a gaze of greedy

---

4. *The final scene of* Faat Kine, *a film discussed later, portrays what we are to infer is the sexual satisfaction of the eponymous heroine by a protracted shot of her toes curling in pleasure.*

insistence (*'insistence gourmande'*). Relations between men and women, in Sembene's account, have more to do with reproduction[5] and reputation.

Xala's particular conundrums result from an expectation that successful men will continue to acquire wives and produce children as proof of their manhood into late middle age. This is why Adja is in such a weak position in terms of the marital economy, while El Hadji, at least a decade and a half her senior, thinks he is in a strong position (even if he discovers differently); why the reproductive life cycles of middle-class men and women diverge so in middle age when polygynous marriage is a normal perk, and 'duty', of success; and why wives necessarily compete for the attentions of their husband, and look to their own advantages: whether of seniority for a first wife, or of youthful attraction for a last wife. Lacking either of these assets, a middle wife is most likely to be suspected of acting from jealousy, as is Oumi. Within this patriarchal arrangement, young women are additionally subject to the status aspirations of their older women kin, like her mother and paternal aunt in N'Goné's case. Even the polygynous husband is accorded some of Sembene's sympathy, or at least understanding, for his plight, dealing with wives, and their relatives, who may squabble and promote the interests of their own children, while having almost no space to call his own, other than, like El Hadji, a grubby

----

5. *At the denouement of the novella, Adja Awa is confronted by a beggar and a mother of twins who demands, 'Who am I?' ... 'Would you say a woman? No. I am an object of reproduction.'*

office and the back seat of his chauffeured Mercedes limousine. Sembene presents the complexity of polygyny, particularly in its urban form, as a social arrangement that is at once economic, emotional, religious, cultural, and status-laden, and contested on all these counts.

kleptocrats

kleptocracy: the rule of robbers.

I n both its book and film versions the plot of *Xala* is impelled by a broad spectrum of thefts, on the part of politicians, police, and pickpockets, who turn out to be, or become, in cahoots with one another. The overture of the film dissects thefts of trust, power, position and money by a neo-colonial African elite spouting ideology entirely at variance with its own behaviour. Such behaviour, the film moves immediately to suggest, is not exceptional but pervades modern Senegalese or at least Dakarois society. There follow three immediate repetitions, none of them in the book version.

First: arriving at the villa of his third wife for their wedding reception, El Hadji nonchalantly throws a handful of coins to beggars
at the gate; a large black military boot (already iconic from the
overture) descends on one coin before the vulnerable, bare hand
of the boy who guides a blind beggar can retrieve it; as the beggar
gestures his annoyance, the coin disappears into the breast pocket
of a military tunic we shall find out belongs to a member of the
Cerbères, or Security Police. This gesture will be reversed in the
film's denouement when a beggar, whose debility prevents him
from flexing his fingers to retrieve dropped coins, adeptly lifts
them by impressing them into the back of his hand. Left to their
ingenuity, the disabled are able in their own ways.

Second: El Hadji's invitees from the Chamber of Commerce take
the opportunity provided by his wedding reception to discuss
business and fix deals. As mentioned in the last section, we listen
in while Kebe, the *Député*, who is also a Board member, negotiates
his cut on a contract with a businessman seeking permission for
a tourism scheme. The *Député* insists on payment in cash rather
than by cheque because he never leaves 'traces' of his affairs,
a sense which includes the spoor a hunter might follow. Their
good-humoured discussion dwells on the theme of the 'honour'
of *hommes d'affaires*, meaning no more in this context than their
complicity in mutual enrichment, a theme to which we shall
need to return. The dependence on tourism, only a decade after
Independence, already strikes Sembene as a particularly demean-
ing type of clientship.

Third: just ahead of El Hadji's arrival at his office on the morning after he has failed to consummate his marriage, a pedestrian is struck down by a car. A crowd forms to gawp, some of whom help to push-start the car which departs apparently with impunity. While distracted by this commotion, a villager just arrived in the city from his drought-stricken village has his bag picked, and all the money raised by the near-destitute farmers for food is stolen. The young pickpocket responsible will go on to become the member of the Chamber of Commerce who replaces El Hadji; his start on the road to riches echoes El Hadji's earlier theft by land-sale from the countryside to establish himself in the city, and it does so as farce more than tragedy, since his first investment from his ill-gotten gains is in a flashy blazer with silver buttons, and an incongruous Stetson straw hat. Theft becomes banal through repetition, almost beyond caricature, as Sembene demonstrates in these two instances that enrich the city at the expense of the countryside, and make feasts for some out of general famine.

It's a dog-eat-dog society in which thieves also become 'victims' in their turn. The novella demonstrates this even more powerfully than the film when the impotent El Hadji is fleeced by a succession of marabouts who sap his assets along with his will, honour and manhood (these several charlatans have to be condensed into the single figure of a parodic marabout/*féticheur* to fit into the narrative time frame of the film). The impotence they are supposed to cure is the upshot of his third marriage, itself revealed in the novel to have been a piece of trickery into which he was enticed by his old acquaintance, the Badiène, eager to settle down her flighty 'daughter', a girl who is unlikely to be the virgin bride she seems. Few of the characters in *Xala* are trustworthy and can be held to their word; appearances regularly deceive.

As our knowledge grows we understand another theft that preceded the entire drama and provides its motive force. El Hadji's ascent from school teacher and firebrand independence activist to trader and pillar of the Chamber amongst the *hommes d'affaires* began with his illicit sale of village land that was vested in the name of his father as chief, though held in trust for the clan. His thefts have to continue to support his lifestyle and that of his dependants: he fails to pay the Société Vivrière Nationale (National Food Board) for rice he sells (in the film to his Mauritanian associate Ahmed Fall) because he has exhausted the proceeds in the expensive business of taking and accommodating his third wife. Living on credit, his cheques start to bounce and he cannot pay either his 'secretary-saleswoman', Madame Diouf, who loyally continues to work until she can afford to do so no longer, or the most constant figure of the entire drama, his chauffeur Modu, who remains until the bitter end to drive the minimal trace of the Mercedes that in the novella is Rama's Fiat coupé, but the film reduces to his own wooden stool that he carries in one hand while he supports El Hadji with the other.[1] El Hadji's associates from

---

1. *The wooden stool is an example of locally-made furniture commonly, like the seating and retail displays made from packing cases, seen at the roadside in Dakar, a further contrast with the* imported *Mercedes.*

a ruler
should not
behave
like
a lizard

the Chamber of Commerce are unfazed by his thefts but greatly inconvenienced when, by drawing cheques on the bank for which he lacks collateral, he brings the credit-worthiness of all of them, from 'His Excellency' downwards, into disrepute.

In a climactic scene back at the Chamber of Commerce, when El Hadji is expelled from the Board, he rails against the criticisms of his colleagues: they are all thieves, all use the same practices; and while the Board denies this truth, the film underlines it when the pickpocket in his sharp clothes and Stetson straw hat takes the place of El Hadji, just as the President and El Hadji had earlier taken those of the colonial figures. So repetition goes with decline: the pickpocket is just a decultured petty criminal, without even El Hadji's claims to upbringing in a chiefly family, western education to become a teacher, or the political consciousness to have been an activist in his youth.

Without production, the city is built from theft, and particularly theft from the countryside: the land stolen by El Hadji, the money stolen by the pickpocket that would have provided the seed to farm it, the relief rice sold under the counter. But the beggars do not steal; and beggars pay their debts. The camera lingers over their commensality, a contrast with the rank consumption of the wedding feast. Getting themselves back to the city from the arid wilderness where they have been dumped by the Cerbères, past the welcoming signpost that greets them with '*Soyez les bien-venus*', the beggars share a modest meal of coffee (Nescafé and condensed sweetened milk vigorously stirred) and fresh-baked bread passed hand to hand to a soundtrack accompaniment of the lute supporting the lilting high-pitched vocal refrain that sympathizes with the poor; the camera pauses to watch the moment when the blind beggar pays promptly for all to eat and drink, declaring he has neither bills nor debts to pay. This same figure, having commented that Serigne Mada, whom El Hadji tried to cheat with a worthless cheque, was a man of his word for retying the *xala*, will refuse money to lift El Hadji's curse of *xala* because the debt he has come to collect goes beyond money to a more primordial code of honour and human connection. For El Hadji, every debt is a money debt, and all relations translate into cash terms. In the end, his is a lonely world without solidarity, loyalty or (at least on his part, so far as we can infer) selfless love. The blind beggar, who is only finally given a name, his village 'brother' rather than a 'brother' member of the Chamber, recalls another notion of social debt owed to inter-personal honour.

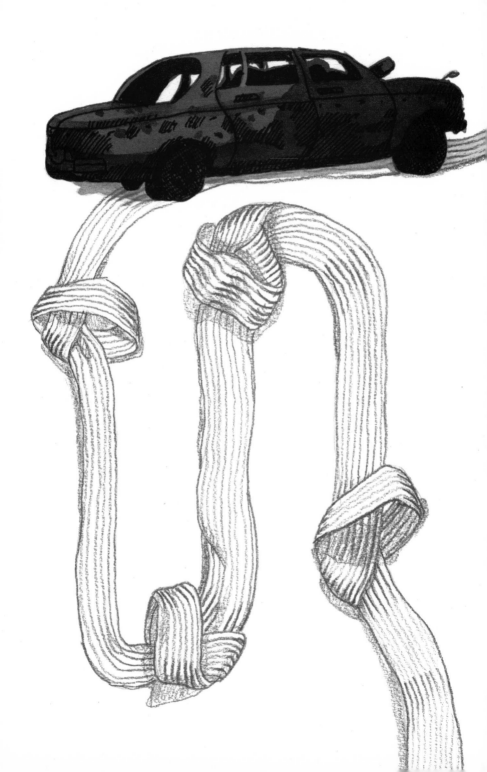

mobilities

*comportment: personal manner,
demeanour and bearing,
including characteristic motion.*

X*ala*, particularly the film as the more mobile narrative vehicle, is fascinated by types of locomotion. The editing is restless, composed from shorter cuts than most of Sembene's films, notably those not set in the city. Characters are defined by how they move, movement being the dynamic dimension of their general bodily appearance. Dress and comportment usually coincide. Instances are easy to recollect: when the post-independence politicians, in their implausibly everyday African attire, take possession of the Chamber of Commerce, they bound up the stone steps with a youthful exuberance entirely absence from their later appearance as measured men, elders in measured suits. Suits – dinner suits or tailored, lounge suits – impose sobriety on the movements of their wearers.

This sense of bounding energy is transferred to the beggars when they set upon their return to the city from the wasteland in which they, as 'human waste', have been dumped. Their determined comportment tells us that the aspirations the politicians once pretended to embody – now betrayed by their western-suited bodies – the beggars truly embody, despite their bodily impairments. The lamest are carried by the more able-bodied and the blind led by the sighted. They are in solidarity with others caught up in the police raid: the robbed peasant, and the street vendor of *Kaddu* (the Wolof-language newspaper) to whom he had been telling his story, the boy who cleans the Mercedes for Modu and suffers a head wound. Sembene frames them heroically mounting a sandy ridge against an expanse of brightest blue sky. The book, which is driven more by individual characters and the relations, often of family, between them, does not ennoble the beggars to this degree. The textual narrative withholds the shock of the beggars as a group until they appear at its denouement when their wounds and diseases are described in lurid detail to evoke the worst nightmare of the new African bourgeoisie. Their stench is fetid; flies swarm around them; and one beggar oozes a trail of slime behind him like a 'slug'. They move like a teeming infestation.

If controlled energy is valued, so also is dignified restraint. The charlatan marabout to whom the President of the Chamber of Commerce refers the impotent El Hadji in the film (who most resembles Papa Jean's marabout in the novella) is a phenomenon of laughter and broad gestures, including an aspersion of water prefiguring the beggars' later expectorations, all of which lead to nothing but ridicule for his wretched patient, sent to his bridal chamber with lotions, and magical accoutrements, commanded to crawl, beast-like, on all-fours, fetish clasped between his teeth, which causes N'Goné to shriek with alarm. Throughout the divination session, El Hadji remains dressed in the formal dinner suit he still wears from his wedding on the previous day. The chauffeur Modu's village marabout, by contrast, is restrained in comportment, and his magic literate, counting his dark prayer beads through prayers and Koranic verses. His remote compound is reached by an arduous journey back to Modu's home during which the Mercedes has to be abandoned forcing El Hadji to eat dust and endure heat on a horse and cart. The cure is carried out on the spot and requires El Hadji to remove his western business clothes entirely. When El Hadji's cheque bounces, and the marabout revokes the cure he invoked – which lasted the single night that, ironically, El Hadji spent in the generous embrace of his second wife – this figure in the whirlwind of El Hadji's descent into nothingness appears as a striding countryman wearing the best of his traditional robes to visit the city; restoring the *xala* requires him only to sit on the pavement and intone almost silently while clicking his prayer beads.

Transport amplifies the qualities of embodiment to which the film directs our attention: most obviously the politicians in the overture to the film exchange their soft shoes and sandals for formal black shoes, over which the camera and soundtrack linger,

everybody will have their turn

and swap walking for luxury limousines always named by their marque. The security forces responsible for order, and violent repression, are indexed to their boots, framed as instruments of aggressive appropriation in the early scene when El Hadji scatters coins to the beggars who have congregated outside the gates to witness the celebrations of his third marriage, an activity that comes to seem more menacing in the light of our later knowledge. Their motor transport consists of military vehicles like the jeep, and the prison wagon that is multiply labelled Cerbères.

The film loves footwear (unusually, for a film, men's footwear) and motor vehicles, and also uses the second to delineate female characters. The third wife, an almost wordless commodity in the film, is mirrored in the small car (a Fiat 127 coupé) on a car carrier, banded with its absurd ribbon – like an 'Easter egg' – that is never unloaded for her to drive (just as she remains metaphorically driverless). Thinking he will be able to consummate his marriage on return from Modu's marabout, El Hadji fingers the ribbons in anticipation. This vehicle is the object of the envy of El Hadji's second wife who demands parity. Whereas, in the film, the liberated Rama, the trouser-wearing, Wolof-speaking, daughter of El Hadji's first wife, rides her moped past the Université de Dakar, the book gives Rama a small car apparently of an identical model to the present given N'Goné by her future husband (underlining the similarities, particularly of age and standing between the new wife and the oldest daughter, as well as the antagonisms between their two inclinations towards modernity). We last hear about this vehicle in the novel as it transports El Hadji, with Modu at the wheel and the bridal mannequin, to the house of his first wife, as his world collapses around his ears.

At various points in the film, vehicles move the plot between places: for instance, the two convoys of the overture, carrying the members of the Board of the Chamber of Commerce and the bride's party to the wedding reception from the Place de l'Indépendance; or the police vehicles which deport the beggars outside the city and hence initiate the long journey they take back to the most intimate of El Hadji's family places; or Ahmed Fall's pick-up truck which leaves El Hadji's Dakar warehouse for the countryside overloaded with new stock. More generally, transport incidents precipitate chains of events: the most obvious example in the film is the motor accident that occurs just before El Hadji arrives at his shop-warehouse for the first time. A small white Renault 4 van knocks down a pedestrian who is injured seriously to judge by the way he is carried off. The car is push-started and allowed to depart by helpful onlookers, preoccupied with the vehicle more than the welfare of its victim; these goings-on create the commotion that distracts the peasant visitor to Dakar who has his bag emptied of the money with which he was sent to buy the essentials for survival by his fellow villagers, and that theft sets up the career of the young pickpocket who will take El Hadji's place in the Chamber of Commerce. These incidents had left only scant traces in the book, for instance, one of the beggars in the denouement recounts that his circumstances were changed by a motor accident very similar to that Sembene has realized in the film.

This emphasis on mobility – or motor force – in the plot, draws our attention particularly to instances of stillness or reduced movement. As El Hadji's circumstances crumble, and his property is seized, there is the absurd spectacle of his Mercedes pushed rather than driven away by the forces of order, each of whom confirms individually to the bailiff, acting on behalf of the Société Vivrière Nationale (National Food Board), that he does not know how to drive it. Not knowing how to drive the Mercedes, recalls the Fiat that N'Goné cannot drive which sits inert, gift-wrapped in ribbons, on the car-carrier, evoking the bridal mannequin, and El Hadji's inability to drive N'Goné herself.'

You are how you move. The film has many styles of walking, beginning with the contrast between how the new political class moved before and after they took possession of the Chamber and swapped their African clothes for the western suits, shoes and attaché cases over which the camera lingered. Initially, El Hadji carries himself upright with self-possession, but his *xala* affects not just the erectness of his penis but his entire bodily posture. He begins to walk more slowly, head bowed, eyes to the ground, like the ageing man he is; the attaché case seems to grow

----

1. *The French verb* conduire *has a different range of senses from its English equivalent 'to drive' which appropriately in this analogy include 'to lead' and 'to conduct'.*

heavier. After his honeymoon night, he cannot even bear to enter *la Mercédès* and Modu has to follow him at the wheel of the car down the road from Villa N'Goné. The only occasion during the remainder of the film when El Hadji will again be comfortable in his own skin is reclining in the back of his Mercedes listening to music after Modu's marabout has cured him of his *xala* (recall that in French *impuissant* elides the related but, in normal speech, distinct English senses of powerless and impotent). But once Serigne Mada revokes his cure, El Hadji groans and visibly deflates to sit on Modu's humble wooden stool, a huddled, speechless, flaccid figure.

You are how you move, but also where you move, and the film delineates several zones of comportment: the Chamber of Commerce on the Place de l'Indépendance, with other government buildings nearby; the banks in the neighbouring area; the residential suburbs (the villas of the three wives, the first two we are told in the book are nearly identical apart from their furnishings, unsurprisingly since El Hadji married his second wife only three years after the first; the third villa is in a more recent residential development); the commercial *quartier* in the shadow of Dakar's Grande Mosquée, where El Hadji has his warehouse-office and where much of the action is initiated by the motor accident and ensuing theft; the villages of the marabouts; and the utterly bleak exile to which the beggars are briefly consigned. Although we do not see the interior of Senegal which is being ravaged by the Sahelian drought of the 1970s, we are aware that this place also is among the movers of the unfolding drama. The countryside stands revealed as the scene of El Hadji's class theft, the act that we learn by the end of the film has produced effects that cascade down to the present as a toxic mixture of environmental disaster meeting the aftermath of land grabs presided over by an uncaring kleptocracy now ensconced in the state. The unseen background is grinding rural poverty. And we are scarcely aware of the *quartiers* of the urban poor, since the beggars do not live there but in the interstices of the world of the rich, like vermin they strive to expel.

Xala, like much of Sembene's art, is fascinated by types of locomotion, journeys, and the relations forged between different kinds of spaces. In its final act, to close a denouement that recapitulates its overture in reverse, the most socially marginalized have imposed their presence at the most secluded of small bourgeois domestic spaces into which El Hadji has been driven: the living room of his senior wife. Like a dying man, El Hadji finds his mobility shrinking to the dimensions of his body. Further movement in the direction both have been pursuing is impossible. When neither El Hadji nor the beggars can draw any closer to the intimate centre of El Hadji's family life, the film, which has been about mobility, closes in immobility with a freeze frame; while in its French original, the novella closes in suspension with three full stops...

fetishism

*fetish: something humanly made
to which inhuman or super-human
properties are attributed.*

etishism, in two senses, has provided a
convenient lens for appreciation of *Xala*.
Sembene's Marxism was well-known,
hence the reasonable anticipation that his
imagery in this film reflects Marx's views
on the fetishistic allure of commoditized
things. Fetishism historically, as has also become well known,
derived in an African context from the Portuguese verb to make;
hence, a fetish as something made, particularly made by Africans,
to which is attributed powers that it lacks in reality. A theory of
fetishism returned to Africa by an African has a sense of etymo-
logical-historical authenticity or familiarity, and this is a source of

potential danger as well as insight. Should we read African fetish-ism proposed by an African marxist literally or ironically or both? And if both, does this imply it is sometimes ironic and sometimes literal, or that it is always both? There isn't an easy answer, which, teasingly, may be the point.

As I noted earlier, the same cast of characters differ not just in their composition and relative importance between book and film, but also in the ways in which they are conveyed to us. The book's more important characters are given biographies and inner thoughts that make sense in terms of these life histories. This would be more difficult to achieve in the film treatment, but far from impossible had Sembene wished to emulate his text. Instead, as the overture announces, characters will be presented as stereotypes, almost masks in the theatrical sense, their significant characteristics composed by assembling attributes into composites, which is also how a great many African masks and masquerades are – to my mind – best interpreted, as an assemblage of still-separately-recog-nizable parts. The film fetishizes more than the novel: its new-elite characters, as Laura Mulvey suggested, seem to have grown a hard shell, or carapace, around themselves in the form of material pos-sessions and adornments, but the appearance of durability of this shell, or masquerade, is illusory.

Another important consideration before we embark on all this concerns Sembene's treatment of African religion, which has not always been fully appreciated by commentators. Senegal is an overwhelmingly Muslim country in which a few sufi brotherhoods, notably those of the Tijani and Murid, wield particular power, not just in religious but also in economic and political affairs. Historically, although this may not remain true indefinitely given currents of Islamic reformism, it has also been a country where variable fusions of Islamic and African notions of supernatural power have been longstanding in the form of *maraboutage*, the techniques wielded by marabouts. In the words of a Senegalese scholar, '*Maraboutage* is a cultural fact and vital social reality to which individuals have constant recourse, particularly when dealing with circumstances that are professional, amorous or conflictual.' Most Muslims in Senegal carry charms for personal protection from malevolent forces and believe in the capacity of others to attack them using such powers. But the style and repertoire of marabouts vary. This becomes important to noticing distinctions the film is making. For instance, the series of marabouts successively consulted in the book is resolved into just two representative figures in the film: the personal marabout-cum-diviner of the President of the Chamber of Commerce, and the marabout from the home village of Modu, the loyal chauffeur. The President's marabout is a striking character made up by Sembene from broad gestures, gales of laughter, and a magical technology that involves reading the signs of things he uses in divination rather than writing per se. He sends El Hadji back to his new wife equipped at some expense with a magical wash, a belt, and a fetish to be gripped between his teeth as he approaches his wife on all fours. Not only is the treatment useless, it terrifies N'Goné who screams with fear as El Hadji approaches her crouching like an animal in pursuit of the prey that she is described as being. The fetish device, with its small bell, is mockingly removed from El Hadji's briefcase when it is emptied to be reassigned to his pickpocket replacement on the Board of the Chamber of Commerce towards the end of film. The most prominent characteristic of the marabout who comes up with this device, so the President tells El Hadji as if this guaranteed his power, is that he is 'expensive, really expensive'. Even though the marabout's self-presentation is superficially 'deep rural', the journey that the President and El Hadji take to reach him is short (to judge by Dupont-Durand being asked to absent himself from the office for only an hour while they undertake the journey, returning apparently unruffled in their dark suits and shoes). Sembene's gaze at this kind of fetishism is withering.

The contrast with Serigne Mada, Modu's marabout is striking. Modu and El Hadji, as we saw, have to embark on a long and, for the haplessly urban El Hadji, tiresome journey back to Modu's rural roots, which he at least continues to respect. There, as the book recounts, they are given water and food (both of which El Hadji unreasonably refuses) and they sleep, Modu happily and El Hadji reluctantly. When they awake and a naked El Hadji is treated, the restrained ritual, by comparison with that performed by the President's marabout, involves his being covered with a cloth from a holy man living in the foothills of the Atlas Mountains, and the recitation of verses from the Koran. In short, this is a literate performance informed by outside Islamic knowledge, and while

Serigne Mada may live deep in the country, he is comfortable in the city, knows perfectly well what a cheque is, and presents himself in Dakar to cash the one El Hadji gave him. When the cheque bounces, in the book version which is the more expansive account of this episode also, the modestly dressed marabout is brought anonymously to El Hadji who fails to honour him by recognizing him and addressing him by name. Recall that this is a society in which name and reputation count, El Hadji's failure to name Serigne Mada foreshadows his failure, only a little later in the narrative, to name the beggar, the clan member his actions thrust into penury. To put it in loosely structuralist terms, that is in terms of opposed statements, if being named by the griot risks the hyper-inflation of reputation and the loss of resources, then anonymity in the eyes of the powerful would be its polar opposite, devoid of wealth transfer.[1]

The reference to status is not incidental here. Recall that El Hadji is described early in the book treatment as a part fusion of European and 'feudal' African, and not simply of European and African. Sembene has in mind here, as often in other works, the characteristics specific to societies in the region including most of Senegal (though not Sembene's own region of birth, if not upbringing, the Casamance) and not just a generalized African identity, let alone a theory of negritude. These societies recognize what have been called 'castes', by loose analogy with India, because like their Indian

----

1. *This is part of the crux of* Borom Sarret, *Sembene's first film, when honour demands that a griot who, uninvited, sings the praises of the impecunious carter's noble family must be paid, even at the cost of his 'patron' being unable to feed his family.*

counterparts there are endogamous, or in-marrying, categories which consist of nobles, griots (musician-historian-praise singers), leatherworkers, metalworkers, fishers and so on. El Hadji is the son of a chief, so his 'feudal' upbringing involves his noble status, whether this is looked at in Senegalese or Marxist terms, or both at once. Noble status gives El Hadji a particular weakness where aspersions on his honour are concerned, and this is in part why the Badiène of the novella version can taunt him into action: to marry N'Goné in the first instance, and to continue to seek a cure to his *xala* so as to take 'possession' of his wife, when part of him wants to be done with the whole business and divorce her, never more so than when he begins to find her ill-educated youth shallow and tedious.[2]

As the film goes on, N'Goné seems increasingly to be, not complemented by but actually replaced by the dressmaker's mannequin which wears the bridal dress, wig, veil, and head band or tiara. The mannequin itself is an interesting assemblage of a standard dressmaker's model with a wig-stand, wickerwork head. The first time we see it, this erotic assemblage is in N'Goné's bedroom, not yet clothed with N'Goné's bridal gown, and juxtaposed to the symbols of sexual intercourse: an upturned mortar ready for pounding. It seems to stand witness as a besuited El Hadji refuses the Badiène's repeated requests to remove his trousers and straddle the mortar while he holds the phallic axe handle (of the book) or pestle (of

----

2. *The early novella* Vehi-Ciosane *(1966) recounts the effects of father-daughter incest made more terrible by the fact of occurring in a family of noble descent* (guel-waar*).*

the film) upright between his legs. The promise of the now clothed bridal mannequin is all that El Hadji retains after his divorce when, in the book version, it like him is driven to his first wife's home by Modu at the wheel of Rama's tiny Fiat coupé. The film symbolically strengthens this denial of masculinity by having the bridal mannequin delivered to Villa Adja by an exaggeratedly effeminate, *homme-femme*, male member of N'Goné's mother's household, who returns it at the same time as making the announcement of N'Goné's divorce from El Hadji. Finally, El Hadji is himself identified with the mannequin when made to wear its, or her, bridal crown.

Until the divorce, the bridal mannequin has occupied a private space, beside the door through which the bride's bedroom chamber is entered. It is the counterpart, or counter-gift, to the husband's gifts exposed in the public space for all to see, some of them supplements to the erotic gift of N'Goné herself. The film merges two distinct spaces in which the bridal reception is held in the book version: the home of N'Goné's parents, and the third villa bought by El Hadji for his new wife. At the first of these,

> In the middle of the main room of the house the husband's gifts were displayed in sets of a dozen each on a trestle table: lady's underwear, toiletries, shoes in various fashions and colours, wigs from blonde to jet black, fine handkerchiefs and scented soaps. The centre-piece was a red casket inside which lay the keys of a car.

The French description of these intimate commodities is more seductively fetishized than the translation conveys.

Au centre de la maison, sur une table de fortune, étaient exposés les cadeaux du mari, à la douzaine par unité: lingerie de corps intime pour femme, nécessaires de toilette, paires de chaussures de modèles et de teintes varies, perruques allant de la blonde à la noir-nuit, mouchoirs fins, savons de toilette. Le clou était les clefs d'une voiture, logées dans un écrin rouge au milieu de cette table.

All the treasures in this tournament of value are displayed on a *table de fortune*, one that has been made from materials that happen, fortuitously, to be available: a cobbled-together infrastructure as a Marxist might note. 'Intimate lingerie for a woman's body', to translate literally, promises something different from 'lady's underwear', and a jet black wig lacks the full connotations of one that is 'night-', or more idiomatically in English, 'midnight-black'. The highlight of the gifts 'exposed', the car keys, are enclosed in a red presentational casket (not vice versa as in the English translation); as the car itself ('*le «coupé-auto-cadeau-mariage»*') is gift-wrapped with a white ribbon, like a 'trophy', or like an Easter egg, a commercialized Christian image of fertility that is oddly appropriate to this westernized wedding ceremony held by Muslims.

The erotic associations are simultaneously elements within a systematic coding of the ceremony into its more and less westernized parts. The bridal attire is clearly western, as is the tiered wedding cake, with its idealized model couple atop, whose dress reminds us of the bridal mannequin. Moreso in the book than in the film, the music is also divided into competing genres belonging to the griots and the 'west', with the second further sub-divided generationally most notably between the tango chosen as the couple's first dance – the most famous of them all, the 'eternal Comparsita' (properly *la Cumparsita*) – and *le jerk* (rock 'n' roll) favoured by the younger crowd (the film hardly explores this distinction because the Etoiles de Dakar provide an updated soundtrack to the wedding reception). The youngsters have provided '*les filles et garçons d'honneur*' in European dress and are anxious to quit the parents' house to attend the reception. A trace of this event remains in the film in the shape of the matching costumes worn by the young people accompanying N'Goné on her arrival at the reception in her own new home. Returning to the book, the family's distinguished older guests are in their traditional robes and concern themselves with the wedding vows and ceremonies, even in the absence of the couple themselves.

The language of the film is saturated with fetishized objects and brands. The (original French, but not English-translated) novella repeatedly specifies Evian as the only brand of mineral water El Hadji will drink; Sembene cannot resist the temptation in the film to ramp up the irony by making it the water brand of choice for El Hadji's Mercedes too, not just to top up its radiator but even to wash it. Consumption of imported mineral water is one of the issues contested by Rama. The list of items of *tubab* culture is long,

*what
one hand
has planted,
another can
pull up*

and we met many of them in the overture. Some are expelled defin-
itively, like the busts of Marianne and Marie-Antoinette, others,
like the military boots and military headgear, make a rapid return
in the same or similar form. Business suits, black leather shoes, and
attaché cases evoke the corruption of the *homme d'affaires*, while
French magazines, clothing and furniture fashions, and other
accoutrements like wigs to cover African hair (by contrast with
Rama's practical hair-styles ranging from short hair to tight plaits)
demonstrate the avid consumerism of the new bourgeoisie, per-
sonified best by El Hadji's second wife, Oumi, and her high-main-
tenance children. Adja and Oumi are seated in a newly furnished
salon at N'Goné's wedding, with sofa, standard lamps and a large,
abstract, modern painting. Again, Sembene pursues his satire to
the ludicrous in the film treatment, so the *nouveaux riches* make
fools of themselves by asking to know what the English call *le
weekend,* and demonstrate their alienation by complaining about
the number of Africans they meet when abroad in Europe, 'negritude really travels!'. While the Minister, attired in dinner suit, picks
his nose and is then at a loss to know how to dispose of his pick-
ings. Still at the reception, Sembene constrasts Adja Awa, chewing
on her dental stick, with Oumi, chewing on the arm (or temple) of
her designer sunglasses.

Any viewer of the film or reader of the book can easily multiply
these examples, and notice analogies to other fetishes. Take language, for instance, the poles of which are furnished by the insistence of the Chamber on 'the purest French expression' – 'even

for insults' – to the adherence of Rama to Wolof even if (in the book) she has to lie to the policeman, who stops her after a traffic offence, by claiming to him that she is unable to speak French. We know that Sembene was sympathetic to the use of African language in place of French, since he financed the Wolof-language newspaper *Kaddu* that is sold in the film. There are indicators of the wide reach of the newspaper: Madame Diouf, El Hadji's secretary-saleswoman, buys a copy, and like other by-standers the *Kaddu* seller is caught up in the police raid that leads to the expulsion of the beggars, and their heroic return. But little in Sembene is wholly devoid of ambivalence. Just as the beggars are not entirely noble in action, so the fetishization of language-medium over message must be questioned, as we see when El Hadji belatedly decides to launch a Wolof-language critique of the Board of the Chamber of Commerce only at the moment of his expulsion from it.

What of the most conventional of African fetishes: wooden carvings? *Xala* the film has two types of sculpted objects that are treated differently. African masks appear on two occasions, but on neither occasion as masquerades: one mask adorns the wall of the President's office when El Hadji is summoned to explain his inability to meet his debts. The President's office inside a modern block is reached by a lift. There El Hadji finds the President ensconced with his adviser, Dupont-Durand, and the camera moves between this *tubab* and the mask on the wall above the President seated at his desk, on which there is a kneeling carved figure, as if to explain that the neo-colonial presence and the Africanist gestures are parts of the same circumstance that is being anatomized. The fact of the mask not being Senegalese only reinforces this sense of alienation from an African past that itself is being fetishized by Europeanized Africans. An African mask appears on a second occasion inside the Chamber of Commerce when the Board members are casting ballots to decide on El Hadji's expulsion. A Yoruba mask is simply turned over to serve as the bowl into which ballots are placed. Not only is this not a Senegalese mask, it is not even being allowed to show its face, while its normally concealed side is used as no more than a receptacle for an imported procedure.

The African masks of *Xala* may not be presented as powerful objects (in the way Sembene had exploited the evocative power of a mask in his earlier film *La noire de...*), but the staff of the blind beggar, who will set in train El Hadji's downfall, is treated quite otherwise. Gorgui Bèye, portrayed powerfully by Douta Seck, the only experienced actor in the film, is led by his staff which has a carved human head, and on occasions is shown almost to float before him. With his staff, Gorgui appears to see more than the sighted. Virginie Andriamirado has drawn attention to the remarkable original poster[3] for *Xala* that was presumably approved by Sembene himself (also adapted for the cover of the current French DVD release of *Xala*). My own interpretation differs slightly from hers. The lower part of the poster image is occupied by a view from the rear of the naked N'Goné, from her lower ribs to her buttocks,

----
3. http://www.newyorkerfilms.com/Xala-%281977%29/1/300/ *and elsewhere on the web.*

as we see her in the film when her new husband approaches her in their bedroom. The word XALA, capitalized, follows the contours of her spine. The image draws our attention not so much to her sexual attraction as to her faceless, almost anonymous fertility, emphasised by a design of rays which emanate from between her legs. A small silhouetted image of a stooped El Hadji, its feet apparently at the epicentre of the rays, besuited and carrying his attaché case, bent at the knees, steps away towards the viewer's right. The larger figure of Gorgui, his staff grasped in his fist and pointing towards N'Goné's stomach, faces the viewer in three-quarter profile. Seen through a Marxist understanding of reproduction the image can be interpreted readily in terms of the revenge that Gorgui promises to extract: El Hadji stole Gorgui's land, the means by which he would have reproduced his family in the countryside; however, Gorgui's retaliation involves disabling El Hadji's phallus, the means of his sexual reproduction with N'Goné, hence the staff, with its anthropomorphic head that orients Gorgui in the world, occupies, or perhaps bars, the place of El Hadji's phallus.

Sembene described his own views on many questions as contradictory, and no still point of equilibrium between the two poles of western and African cultures is obvious in the film, not least because these poles of western-European-*tubab*-Frenchness, and African-Senegalese-Wolofness are at once both expansionary and prone to the essentialization implied by fetishism, that is of attributing them qualities that may not be intrinsic at all. Although some commentators suggest otherwise, to my mind none of the characters appears to be wholly endorsed by Sembene, unless perhaps the chauffeur Modu who is able to remain loyal to both El Hadji and Serigne Mada, and to feel at home both in the city, where he drives his master's Mercedes, and in the countryside, where he drinks, eats and sleeps serenely. El Hadji himself is avowedly an unsuccessful synthesis in Sembene's eyes, for all that he attempts to redeem himself as a Wolof speaker at the end of the film story. Rama may be the shape of the future, and one commentator has suggested she is Sembene's voice, but she has rhetorically to reject all cultural aspects of western influence, even if it means lying about her ability to speak French and misrecognizing the exotic origins of much of her own brand of modernity. Adja Awa has largely turned her back on aspects of a Western outlook she must have embraced as Renée, but she has done so at the cost of losing connection to the sensuous aspects of life. Oumi, by contrast, has rejected most of her African heritage, assuming she ever had much, but has become a shallow consumer. We could go on anatomizing the imbalance in each character's relationship to Senegal's and Dakar's complexly Franco-Wolof, or Euro-African history. There is no obvious still point or clear spot for Sembene's characters to occupy comfortably. The restlessness of the film's imagery – maps, clothes, poster images, documents in French and Wolof – and of its music, deny the viewer any sense of stillness, just as the last freeze-frame of the film, or in its slightly different way the conclusion of the novella, denies its viewer/reader the sense of narrative closure.

hommes d'affaires: *businessmen, or, perhaps what in English are called entrepreneurs!*

t the denouement of the story, El Hadji is told by the peasant whose bag had been picked clean outside his store, that his loss had been the greater of the two of them: of his dignity, of his honour and of his manhood, and only the last of these could be restored through the humiliation of being spat upon, naked, by what El Hadji considers the dregs of society while his first wife and family look on. What dignity and honour did he have to begin with?

There would appear to be two answers here. One is hereditary entitlement, and the other an acquired attribute that El Hadji claims for a status. His hereditary claim comes from being the son of a clan chief, but this is a position he abuses in order to rob the very people for whom he should have cared. The second claim derives from his membership of a new *evolué*, civilized, French-speaking bourgeoisie with a lifestyle supported by being *hommes d'affaires*, a status that is claimed by some of the story's characters while simultaneously being ironized by their creator, Sembene. Quite what this little phrase is supposed to imply is a recurrent preoccupation of the story. To return to an episode in the film (but not book) that takes place during the wedding reception when Kebe, the *Député*, is approached to discuss a tourist project by a businessman who is seeking his assistance in gaining government permission to proceed: the businessman offers a 10% kickback, which the *Député* argues up to 15%, refusing a cheque and demanding cash in hand (*compte comptant*) on the basis that he leaves no '*traces*' of his affairs. A slapped handshake is made under the rubric '*Parole d'hommes d'affaires*'? roughly 'Businessman's word?' to which the affirmative response is, '*Parole d'hommes d'affaires*'! Between whom is this word good? Only the two parties who collude in a malpractice that amounts to the robbery of their society, another instance of klepto-governance. As we shall see, the denouement of the book provides the occasion for El Hadji to respond to accusations about the morality of his own behaviour by denouncing the flattering self-image of *hommes d'affaires*, who in reality are simply neo-colonial flunkies.

Failure to recognize or to name people reflects not only on the honour and dignity of those who go unnamed, but also reveals the dishonourable negligence of anyone who does not pay personal attention to his fellows. Even asked directly – 'Do you know who I am?' – El Hadji does not recognize Serigne Mada when the marabout returns to tell him that his cheque has bounced and hence the *xala* he has lifted will be re-invoked. The book adds an extra emphasis to this when the marabout specifically requests Modu not to announce him to his boss, so that El Hadji not only fails to recognize Serigne Mada but goes further in his misrecognition to ask that Serigne Mada be sent a message by this intermediary 'relative' asking for further help in his time of difficulties. The failure to recognize Serigne Mada prepares us for a worse failure when El Hadji is again challenged – 'Do you recognize me? Certainly not!' – by the leader of the beggars who also anticipates the reply. The enormity of this misrecognition, and the several dimensions of forgetting it represents, prove to have set in train virtually all the events we have witnessed. The beggar is a Bèye, a family member of El Hadji, whose claims to family land, in a chiefdom the book specifies as Diéko or Jéko,¹ were wilfully ignored, even to the extent of silencing his protest by throwing him into prison. This was possible because El Hadji's father was the chief, the person most responsible for protecting the interests of his people, but also the person in whose name the land became registered. Name

---

1. *Samba Gadjigo, in his biography of Sembene's peripatetic early years, explains that Diéko was one of the plots of land on the peninsular allocated to Sembene's people, the Lebu, that was alienated by his family for profit.*

and title are inexorably linked. The heretofore anonymous petty thief who steals the villagers' money from the man they have sent to town to buy them food, is identified by name, as 'Monsieur' Thieli, three times as he is admitted to membership of the Chamber of Commerce. Commentators agree that 'Thieli' is a bird of prey or carrion bird of some sort, but disagree about which one. An ornithological source specifies not the vulture or eagle, as suggested, but the black kite (*milvus migrans*), a bird of prey that, like Monsieur Thieli, circles on the thermals before swooping on small prey that it has spied.[2]

For a man to be a man of honour, and of name, is also to be a man of his word (a later Sembene film is named for its protagonist, *Guelwaar*, after the warrior-noble status in Wolof). Although not rich, Serigne Mada and the beggar Gorgui Bèye are both men of their word. Serigne Mada promises El Hadji that he will revoke the cure for his *xala* should he not be paid, and the beggar promises revenge for his loss of land status. Both follow through unrelentingly on these promises. El Hadji, by contrast, lies, particularly when trying to borrow money from the bank or his business associate Ahmed Fall. Money and the marketplace have corrupted him.

----

2. *Gugler and Diop translate* thieli *as vulture, although this is not the term (*tan*) found in Wolof dictionaries. The well-known Youssou N'Dour song title 'Thiely' is usually translated as eagle. The identification as black kite is from:* http://wolofresources.org/language/vocab/birds.htm. *The Collins' Field Guide describes the black kite as 'A scavenger; often in great numbers about towns and villages' ... its 'stick nest lined with rags and other trash', which all seems appropriate to Monsieur Thieli.*

*the lion
will not be
denied
his desire
for want of
courage*

The beggar and the marabout are both perfectly competent in the world of money (recall that Serigne Mada warns El Hadji that he understands what a cheque is, and by implication that cheques are not reliable promises since banks can refuse to honour them) but understand these payments as parts of an older economy of inter-personal honour and mutual responsibility.

Homme d'affaires is not the only French phrase or term ironized by Sembene. Even the title *Monsieur* is reproached for its sense of Europeanized one-upmanship. The car-washer thinks Modu a good client because his employer, El Hadji, is a '*Monsieur*'. One of Oumi's children is branded a '*Monsieur*' for complaining about the need for him to take public transport in Dakar, as if he was living there as a Frenchman might, and as the new Senegalese bourgeoisie does. This is the sense of '*Monsieur*' applied three times to the pickpock-et-turned-*homme d'affaires* '*Monsieur*' Thieli as he takes El Hadji's place among the worthies in the Chamber of Commerce. By the end of the film all the titles, '*Monsieur Le Président*', '*Monsieur le Ministre*', '*Monsieur le Député*, even '*Honorables collègues*' have become difficult to hear at face value, all have become hollow from the loss of value caused by their over-use by kleptocrats.

Names are not just labels. Naming practices are fraught with haz-ard. Not to be recognized by name is an offence to personal hon-our. But to have a name is also dangerous: praise-singers must be rewarded so the name is not tarnished, and patrons must look after their clients. Names and titles, the currencies of renown, engage in spirals of expenditure as reputation and aspiration chase one another's tails. A weak character like El Hadji is easily drawn into this vortex of reputational inflation and deflation. Once there escape is difficult. Professional wrestling, of which many Senegalese are such avid fans, is a public theatre of reputational flux. Both fighters strut their stuff and are medicated at enormous and publicly appreciated expense by their marabouts before their fans for hours on end as they prepare for the bout. But at the, usually sudden, end of their encounter when one of them is abruptly vanquished the jubilation of the winner and his entourage was, at least to this viewer, as nothing compared to the utter deflation and public desolation of the loser, escorted from the arena like a man mortally wounded. Loss of renown is devastating to them, as it is also to El Hadji in the story of *Xala*.

soundscapes

xalam: *the African lute.*

embene imagined complex soundscapes for *Xala*, not just the one he realized in the film version but also that he described in the novel. Not the whole of the soundscape is musical, but let's begin there.

The contrast between Western and African music is only the start of the set of differences at work. Take the wedding party as described in the novel. Its first venue is the wedding ceremony that El Hadji does not himself attend: this takes place at the home of N'Goné's parents (which we do not witness as film viewers, since like him we remain in the Chamber of Commerce while El Hadji announces his wedding is taking place). The female griots are there to sing the praises of distinguished guests and the couple. Eventually, the cavalcade sets off to the beat of car horns. At N'Goné's villa, the dance proper kicks off with a tango, the 'eternal' *Cumparsita*, when El Hadji takes his new wife onto the floor to begin festivities that are soon taken over by the younger set. By late in the night *le Jerk* (rock 'n' roll) alternates with *la Pachanga* (an upbeat Cuban dance style) when only the young people remain on the dance floor and the band gives its all in soul style.

While there is a female griot in the (conflated) film version of this scene and, as in the book, she wears banknotes pinned to her blouse and ululates her approval of El Hadji's bridal gifts, the contrasts between genres of music are not particularly apparent at the celebration because the house band is the *Etoiles de Dakar* playing in an early version of the *mbalax* (the synthesis of upbeat Western, particularly black American, dance styles with Senegalese drumming) for which they would be celebrated with their lead vocalist Youssou N'Dour. The lead singer of the band line-up that appears in *Xala* is apparently Pape Djibril, also known as 'Chéri Coco' after his most famous song, and not Youssou N'Dour himself as has been widely believed (not least because of the resemblance between the two men when young). Sembene chose a successful, and more modern, synthesis of western (in part African-derived) and African musical styles for his filmed representation, whereas the novel had strongly contrasted the two and then sought another contrast in the age-related preferences of the older guests for tango and the younger for rock 'n' roll. The sources of *mbalax* indicate just how difficult it is to stabilize a simple distinction between western and African as if fusion was a single historical event.

The broader contrast drawn between musical genres in both book and film, however, pits commercialized music against the song or 'blues', accompanied on the wailing *xalam* or lute, of the beggar himself (in the book) or one of the beggar's companions (in the film). The song marks the power of the people, never more so than when it strikes up as El Hadji confides his *xala* to the President the morning following his frustrated wedding nuptials. This music draws El Hadji to the window of his store after which, his anger rising, he asks the President to rid him of the beggars who are a stain on the country's independence. As the book observes, no-one but El Hadji is affected so deeply by this song, a clue to the source of his sexual distress. The President immediately telephones 'Math', presumably the familiar form for Mathieu, the European chief of security not named otherwise, asking him to act against this threat the beggars pose to the country's tourism.

Sembene explained the lyrics of the beggars' song at some length in terms worth quoting since most viewers, like me, will not be able to understand the Wolof lyric which has not been subtitled. His glosses help to unpack a message that might have remained opaque to a non-Wolof audience even if it had been subtitled.

99

It's a sort of popular song that I wrote myself in Wolof. In one sense, it calls to revolt, to the struggle against injustice, against the pow-ers-that-be, against the leaders of today who, if we do not get rid of them, will tomorrow be trees which are going to overrun the place and have to be cut down. The songs are tied in with the deeds and gestures that I have written. They did not come from folklore. I had thought at the start to have them translated, but in the end I gave up the idea because it is unnecessary for a European public.

It is the allegory of a kind of lizard, a lizard who is a bad leader. When he walks in front and you behind, he kills you while saying you want to murder him. When you walk as tall as he does, he kills you while saying: "You want to be my equal." When you walk in front of him he kills you while saying: "You want to profit from my good luck." The song says we have to think very seriously about these leaders who resemble this animal and get rid of them. It ends something like this: "Glory to the people, to the people's rule, to the people's government, which will not be a government by a single individual!"

Joseph Gugler's collaborator Oumar Cherif Diop translated Sembene's lyric from the soundtrack in verse form, also revealing the development of the song alongside the film narrative:

(Outside El Hadji's shop before the beggars are deported)
A ruler should not be like a lizard.
The lizard's character is no good.
If you follow him, he complains that you are stepping on his tail.

If you walk side by side with him, he questions your pretence to be his equal.

And if you walk ahead of him, you hear him say, you are scaring away my insects.

Instead of crying, you have to find a solution for your problems.

The cursed ones are those whose offspring are worthless.

For everything there is a season.

Everybody will have their turn.

The lion cannot be deprived of his desire for lack of courage.

(En route to the denouement at Villa Adja Awa)

The lion is courageous.

The lion is honest.

The lion cannot be deprived of the object of his desire for lack of courage.

The soundtrack to the story of *Xala* is not only instrumental, or indeed musical. There is a continuum between acoustic and mechanical music: from drums and *xalam*, to amplified music, to the beat of the mechanical fetishes. The rhythmic horns of the wedding procession are described in the novel as producing a moving 'mechanical serenade' for the bride. Whereas the sirens of the Presidential cavalcade on its way to the wedding celebrations fill an ominous quiet once the celebratory drumming of the overture to the film has been silenced. Like the crunch of military boots, this is the sound of the transition to despotism. The banal 'Oriental chimes' that announce visitors to Villa Adja take on an odd cadence when the caller is a security guard who comes upon the extraordinary events unfolding as the beggars take over the family's living quarters.

for everything there is a season

Most striking of all is the contrast between the sound-shapes made by French and Wolof languages in *Xala*, the strong consonants of the second feeling integral – perhaps not only to a non-speaker of it – to the forceful impact on the narrative made when the action switches into Wolof. This impact is inflected by gender, generation and class, so that the significance of code-switching cannot be generalized. For instance, while the elite men generally communicate in French with their peers, their wives more typically speak Wolof to one another and also, in the case of El Hadji's wives, to their husband. Adja speaks in Wolof to her daughter Rama, while Oumi briefly addresses herself to her daughter Mariem in French. El Hadji addresses all his children, but not his wives, in French, which only Rama refuses to reciprocate. While commentators have been tempted to find a strong statement about language policy in Sembene's film, notably in Rama's refusal to speak French and in the persecution of the salesman of the Wolof-language periodical *Kaddu*, the film portrays a more nuanced everyday code-switching that is alert to the situational significance of the idiom used.

Language and music, the mechanical and the acoustic, and the background hum of traffic and crowds, all contribute to the complexities of the post-colonial, urban soundscape

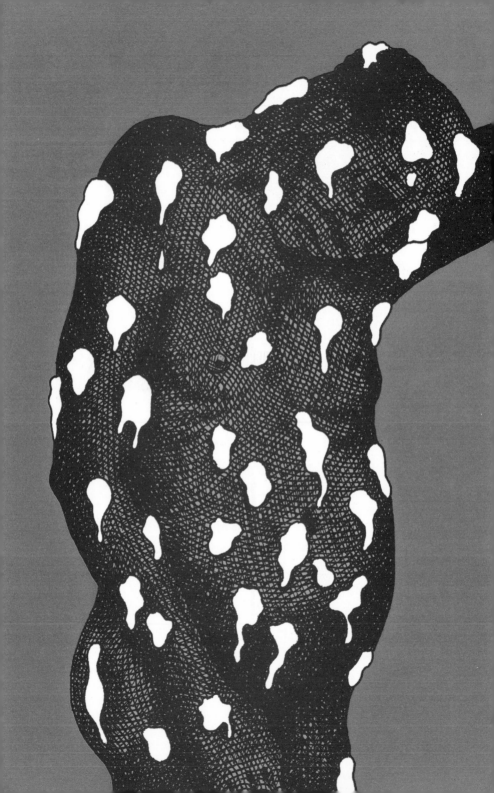

denouement

denouement: etymologically a French unknotting dénouement, *but in English a conclusive knitting together.*

The old French idiom used by Sembene to mean 'to afflict with impotence' is, as noted earlier, *nouer l'aiguillette*, literally to knot the cord that holds in place an item of dress, apparently a codpiece in this instance. To undo such a curse is *dénouer l'aiguillette*, which makes it appropriate that the issues broached in what I called the film's overture should find some resolution in the ending for which English conventionally borrows the French term *dénouement*, or unknotting. As we shall see, the action of the ending unfolds in the same locations as the beginning, and in doing so draws us to a particular reading of *Xala* as a story about corruption and corruptibility: about humans who make and become waste; who waste their own and others' lives. The fight against stench and contamination is unrelenting and unavailing; this society produces 'left-overs' (*restes, bribes*) as fast as it is able to clean them up. As the beggar tells El Hadji – addressing him with the familiar *tu* – just before the climax of the final scenes,

> *Toute ta fortune passée ... était bâtie sur la filouterie. ... Et quand notre*
> *nombre est quantitivement gênant, vous appelez votre police pour ...*
> *- Pour nous éjecter comme des matières fécales.*
> [All your past fortune ... was built on fraud ... And when our numbers
> become a nuisance you call the police to ...
> - To discharge us like so much faecal matter.]

At the graphic denouement of the plot, the worst pollutions Sembene's imaginative powers can conjure up are summoned into the only sanctum of peace and purity presented to us, the home of El Hadji's first wife Adja, the one place that has stood apart from El Hadji's decline, not least because it does not belong to him. This is the haven of his virtuous, loyal and long-suffering – but perhaps a little too sanctimonious, hence friendless – wife. By the end, the corruption of his decline encompasses her home as well.

The novella and film provide complementary reflections on waste with similar narrative arcs. To appreciate these we need to trace them over the entire story. Recall that, at the outset, on leaving the Chamber of Commerce, El Hadji's first stop was to collect his senior wife from her villa which is evoked with the hypernormality of David Lynch's hometown America. As described in the book, Villa Adja Awa Astou is in an exclusive, cleanly, residential area of Dakar with surfaced roads, hedged with *flamboyants* or flame trees, bathed by garden sprinklers, its entrance bell a muffled oriental chime, furnished with restrained taste (in comparison to Oumi's villa), a home for children committed to their education. Cinematically speaking, it almost cries out for violation! El Hadji's second stop is to collect his second wife, so that the three of them can make their way to the third villa, that of the new wife, where the lavish wedding reception is taking place.

Descriptions of stench and rottenness, as well as attempts at cleansing and disinfecting, now come fast. Take the wedding celebration. By the time El Hadji parted from his business cronies to take possession of his new wife we are told of their fetid breath (*l'haleine fétide*) and belches that smelt of rotting meat (*rots empuantis*).[1] When he left the villa the next morning, his marriage unconsummated, the garden was strewn with the detritus of the feast and 'clouds of flies were swarming'.[2] In both film and book, El Hadji next makes his way to his warehouse-cum-office in the commercial district of Dakar just as his elegantly attired secretary-saleswoman, Madame Diouf, is 'flytoxing' the premises in her fight against the flies, cockroaches, and geckos which invade walls

---

1. *These are weakened in the English translation to 'his breath smelt' and 'smelly burps'.*

2. *At least this seems to me a more forceful rendering of* 'des essaims de mouches voltigaient' *than the rather bland 'there were flies everywhere'.*

that the book tells us are so damp and pungent that she uses two tins of air freshener or disinfectant a week. In the film her adversaries include human waste. Having sprayed her office because it 'smelt bad', she trips daintily on impractical shoes into the road outside, a bottle of disinfectant in hand, to sanitize a bowlful of grey liquid, presumably no worse than washing-water poured into a drain-cum-pothole in the road by the local woman who had headloaded it there. The gesture was pointless, because as soon as that bowlful was made safe for civilization a bucketful of more alarming, lumpy, liquid, carried by another '*bonne femme*', followed it into the hole. These actions are the preamble to our first meeting in the film version with the beggars as a group; the blind beggar, and some other individuals, were in the crowd outside Villa N'Goné during the wedding reception scene, but not obviously as members of a group. The beggars' arrival is signalled on the soundtrack by the plaintive *xalam* or lute. On crutches, propelled by their hands, or dragged along on their bottoms, they congregate outside the shop. In the book version, there is only a solitary beggar until he is dramatically augmented at the denouement, but his singing is described as '*bribes monotones*', repetitive scraps, like undiscarded leftovers from meals, that agitate no-one but El Hadji, who has him removed by the police only for him to return some weeks later to the same 'dirty' place that must have suited him. His reappearance occurs immediately after the washer boy has complained to Modu about his paltry level of remuneration for washing the Mercedes, which is particularly grubby following the trip to the countryside to visit the marabout Serigne Mada.

Here is a leitmotif in both textual and cinematic versions that is too regular to be accidental. Allusions to dirt or rubbish routinely prefigure the appearance of the novella's beggar or the film's group of beggars. In the novella, the rounds of the rubbish collectors twice presage the arrival of the beggar, '*la benne des éboueux passaient*', 'the rubbish carts passed by', or before the culminating appearance of the beggars en masse, '*La benne des éboueux collectait des ordures du matin, faisant escale devant chaque maison*', 'the rubbish cart collected the night soil, making a stop in front of each house'. The threats of the socially undesirable and the threat of pollution from waste are elided.

Stench is additionally an attribute of age. The Badiène notices that El Hadji himself is beginning to smell rotten with age and tiredness. Not only male but particularly female charms are depicted as susceptible to age: in her thirties, El Hadj's first wife is accused of having the skin of an old fish. Ageing in itself is construed as rotten-ness in relation to sexuality.

The first time we arrive with El Hadji at his office-warehouse after he has discovered he is suffering from *xala*, he summons the President of the Chamber of Commerce by telephone and, in the course of their conversation about the President's marabout, asks him also to arrange the removal of the '*déchets humains*' outside his shop who are an unhygienic blot on the country's independence and, as the President agrees, also a hindrance to the development of tourism. Following the telephone call to the European

head of security, a black maria arrives, multiply labelled CERBÈRES
– capitalization being the alphabetic equivalent of a siren – as
a kind of police equivalent of the rubbish-cart, and the head of
security oversees disposal of this human 'matter out of place' in
a wasteland far outside the city from which, as we noted earlier,
they return painfully, on foot or by whatever form of locomotion
their particular disability permits some of them. Underlining their
solidarity, at times the most disabled are carried.

'*Déchets humains*', or human waste: the phrase used particularly
of – given this is not a polite film we do not have to beat around
the bush – shit and piss, the end-products of the human digestive
system. Throughout history, authorities have wanted cities to be
made safer – at least for themselves – by eliminating or quarantin-
ing the waste products they attract and produce; and this effort
has everywhere been only partly successful. Does the dynamic of
our first meeting with the beggars help explain what happens the
last time we see them? Why is El Hadji's manhood to be restored
by the humiliation of being spat upon by beggars, some of them,
the novella adds, leprous? This is not the benevolent aspersion of
blessings in the medium of water or beer – a dew-like spraying –
but its contrary: phlegm hawked up from the depths of rasping
lungs and gobbed in greyish lumps that run down El Hadji's face
and body, a highly contemporary gesture of disgust rather than an
analogy with some supposed ancestral practice.

But let's delay a moment before this thought to consider its contrary. There are occasions when the cloying sense of filth around Dakar is temporarily relieved, by cool wind or dry heat, or by distance. For instance, in the novel when El Hadji has Modu drive him to the lighthouse on the taller of the Mamelles ('breasts', the proper name of the rounded hillocks) on the northwest of the Presqu'île, or peninsular, at the southwestern tip of which Dakar sits, he feels himself cleansed by the breeze as he looks towards central Dakar sparkling in the distance; or when, driving into the interior to meet Modu's marabout, Serigne Mada, where pure water and well-prepared food are available in a parched landscape, albeit Modu and not El Hadji is best able to appreciate them, and both fall into deep sleep. The very mention of divorce from N'Goné summons an iodine-laden sea breeze. The troubling smell that haunts *Xala* is an urban stench that is peculiarly offensive to new African bourgeois sensibilities.

The denouement to *Xala* depends on a series of reversals which, given the doublings at the heart of the story's composition, and the conventions of allegories with moral messages, should be unsurprising. At the outset of the story we are introduced to the locations that make up El Hadji's life: there is the Chamber of Commerce, the very summit of his ascent (literally up its stone steps) as an *homme d'affaires*; then Modu drives him to Villa Adja Awa and Villa Oumi, to pick up his first two wives, and on to Villa N'Goné for the wedding celebrations for his third wife; after his wedding night, Modu takes him to the office-cum-warehouse where El Hadji built his fortune. The denouement literally runs these scenes backwards, and this reversal is triggered by El Hadji being summoned to explain his inability to cover his debts to the office of the President on an upper floor of a central Dakar office block. The camera remains with the departing El Hadji as he enters the lift: we watch his back reflected in the lift-carriage's mirror, and though we cannot see his face we join him in what feels like a descent in real time as events march on behind his back. We know what he does not: that the President is telephoning to foreclose his last hope of financial salvation. El Hadji is heading confidently to raise a bridging loan from the Banque Internationale pour l'Afrique Occidentale (the name is that of a real bank which had a Paris head office), but this sense of falling tells the viewers that the game is already over. El Hadji will be expelled from the Chamber of Commerce; what assets remain in his warehouse, or in the form of his vehicles, are seized by his creditors (with slight differences between the book and film versions that need not detain us); his third wife divorces him, leaving only the mannequin as her trace; his second wife moves out of her villa before its furnishings and contents can be seized by the bailiffs; El Hadji is left a sojourner in his first wife's house with a bridal mannequin and a stool all that remains of his wealth. We are reminded of what a variety of characters have voiced throughout the story, that what is done can be undone, 'what one hand has planted, another can uproot'. (*'Ce qu'une main a planté, une autre peut ôter'*, on that occasion the sentiment of the Badiène's friend who brought a cockerel to stain the sheeting with blood on the morning of the fruitless nuptials.)

The beggars who were out of place even on the pavements outside El Hadji's shop, or Villa N'Goné, have to be accepted willingly into his most private of spaces, the house of his first wife and her children. The description of the salubrious character of this road is repeated as it becomes the setting down which the troop of beggars will propel themselves, trailing insects and a fetid smell in their wake. One beggar picks up coins from the pavement by pressing them so they adhere to the back of his hand, a reversal of the security guard's pre-emptively placing his boot on a coin that El Hadji had thrown to the beggars outside N'Goné's villa at his wedding reception. Entering Adja Awa's home, and terrifying her maid, the beggars consume or destroy the imported foods and drinks in the family's refrigerator and mock the bridal costume and veil that stands, fetishistically as a part for the whole, for his third wife. El Hadji has to refuse the assistance of the security officer who is told that the beggars are his guests; the guard can respond only that he respects owners' freedom to do as they wish on private property.

Finally, El Hadji must undress and, in an act of voluntary abjection, submit to the beggars spitting on his unclothed body. The innermost human waste of beggars, who themselves are human waste, is splattered on the naked body of their abuser, divested of his western costume, in the most intimate of his domestic spaces. This is as dramatic a reversal of their expulsion from the urban space as can be imagined. As a container, each body is analogized to the city, each leaking its stickier, that is to say more adhesive waste products, and recycling them as a weapon against privilege.

The beggars' sputum is not just intimate human waste, but potentially disease-bearing, as the book makes more apparent than the film when El Hadji is told that the disease of his class is contagious and collective, not simply an individual misfortune, like that of his assailants. Finally, El Hadji is feminized in his humiliation by having his young bride's wedding crown removed from the mannequin and placed on his head. In the film this act is performed, grinningly, by one of his menials, the man who previously washed El Hadji's Mercedes for the chauffeur Modu. El Hadji is made into the mannequin, the inert spectre that has haunted him since his wedding night. In the book version, El Hadji is crowned only after he is entirely naked and covered in sputum. In its final three sentences, the English version describes how,

> The man who had taken the wedding crown placed it on El Hadji's head.
> The tumult grew louder.

> Outside the forces of order raised their weapons in the firing position.

Which differs in slight but significant ways from the French original,

> Celui qui avait ravi la couronne de marriage la posa sur la tête d'El Hadji.
> Le tumulte grandissait.

> Dehors, les forces d'ordre manipulaient leurs armes en position de tir...

The French more than the English suggests something close to a symbolic 'ravishment' of El Hadji, or of his marriage (since Sembene could have chosen to use the phrase 'bridal crown' (*la couronne de mariée*) had he wished.

In its ending, as in its beginning, the film departs slightly from the novella. The action of the forces of order (not 'law and order') who prepare their guns to shoot is suspended by three stops (...) that are omitted in the English translation. The implied question is, 'Will they shoot?' The film foregrounds other ambiguities, since we end on a freeze frame of the spectacle of El Hadji's emasculated body perhaps being restored its manhood by his total degradation, by accepting the waste he has caused (...) but can we believe the beggars' sticky exudation removes El Hadji's *xala*? And if it does, can it remove what *xala* has meant to the film beyond an inability to achieve an erection? The beggars are entirely male in the film, and predominantly male in the novella. As well as El Hadji's family, they have attacked the innocent housemaid of the Villa Adja Awa. Can manhood be restored by such men? The freeze frame withholds a definitive response, but either way this is a profoundly ambivalent outcome for any reading that wants to reconcile Sembene's marxist and feminist agendas comfortably.

last *word*

abjection: the condition of being cast out and into abasement.

Xala, *in both its filmed and textual treatments, is not incidentally preoccupied with dirt and pollution but focused on pollution as a moral challenge. As the particular vehicle of these concerns, the beggars are experienced as the worst forms of pollution imaginable to the new bourgeoisie: as everything that stands in the way of their aspirations to be modern, civilized, evolved, developed, healthy and presentable. The revelation of the film is that this underclass has been produced by the very means of modernization, and that it is particularly created in the city by processes which begin with exploitation of the countryside* *and of its powers of reproduction and reverberate through indiscriminate repression. The beggars are the bourgeoisie's by-products and leftovers. It is a particularly urban and modern, and class-informed pollution both in its causes and its perception, so not a universal in any simple sense.*

Members of all societies are liable to moralize about social categories in terms of pollution beliefs, but the strength of this concern is highly variable. As noted earlier, most societies in what is now Senegal would have had what are loosely called in an African context 'castes'. That is, categories to which people belonged by birth, and within which they married, that were endowed with the powers to fulfil particular tasks on behalf of the rest of society: working in iron or other metals, making pottery, recalling family histories when singing the praises of noble patrons ... and so on. The chiefs also formed a distinct stratum of society. The powers of artisans and artists carried a threat of pollution to others who did not share them, and the bearers of the powers were called (at least in Mande) by a term open to construal as those who should have been thrown away. Given that El Hadji is himself of a chiefly family, there is a strong possibility of there being some degree of conceptual continuity between traditional and modern notions of pollution. But to over-emphasise this would be to underestimate the degree to which post-independence Dakar was a new kind of society, its pollution ideas generated from its particular experience of an elite class in formation differentiating itself from those now fallen to the bottom of the social pile, but who would recently have been intimate acquaintances: kin, friends and neighbours. The fact of this experience occurring in an increasingly dense urban space must also be significant, since the new bourgeoisie was, in practical terms, using its financial resources to expand residential separation on a colonial model, all the while doing this in terms of a claim to promote and represent African interests.

Associations between filth and morality are comparable universally (by definition), but they are not on that account identical. The Dakar case is a characteristic type of association produced where the cultural differentiation of new class elites in terms of purity and pollution has occurred in a context of rapid urbanization on the basis of inadequate infrastructure, notably sewerage, insufficient formal employment to absorb the exodus from the countryside, and rapid polarization of wealth and political standing accompanied by residential separation. From this violence arises an intensive attention to and intense anxiety about pollution that finds its expression both in more traditional idioms, and in French-Senegalese cultural terms that, particularly on the Dakar peninsular, are longstanding and validate French language, civilization and citizenship, even in the immediate aftermath of formal decolonization. The dirty and polluted are not only the abjected of the society but also the abjected elements of the self. Renewal commonly takes the form of cleansing the environment, as at once a practical, aesthetic and ritual activity. Over a decade after the release of Xala, for a period between the late 1980s and early 1990s, Dakar was made over by a movement called SET, for which Youssou N'Dour (this time really him) provided the world with a soundtrack. Young people devoted themselves to the beautification of their city which was cleaned and decorated with public artworks. Slightly earlier, I had been present during the 'War

Against Indiscipline' or 'WAI' in Nigeria, which was a military-led (and militarily-inspired) programme of collective renewal that included collective public cleansing works. For a while, this conception, and its T-shirts, were popular, though a vogue for forced labour soon tends to fade from fashion. It would not be difficult to multiply examples of cleansing in reaction to the sense of pollution, notably in Sierra Leone and Rwanda under post-war reconstruction. In West Africa public pollution has been strongly, and diversely, related to accusations of corruption, both polluting in itself and polluting in its consequences, whether these are ecologically unsound practices that are officially con-doned (as another track on the same Youssou N'Ndour album alleges), or cleansing facilities left unbuilt.

In Xala, *abjection is complicated by being potentially a reaction to African heritage, seen from the perspective of western standards. Sem-bene's narrative seems to search for viable solutions to the dilemma of embodying both African and Western identities, but fails to come up with entirely convincing examples. Sembene does not buy Africanity, negritude, or 'Authenegrafricanitus' as he will later satirize them (in* Le dernier de l'empire); *they are inversions of Western values rather than escapes from them. But Sembene does endorse African lan-guages, African self-presentational styles, African art forms and Afri-can identities. He does not reject Western technology, but he mocks the fetishization of it. Sembene is after all a proponent of a very expensive (predominantly though far from exclusively) western art form, the his-tory of which he knows well. Sembene wanted to make films for cinema in order to reach African audiences wider than those for his writings.*

*instead
of crying,
you have
to find
a solution
for your
problems*

Yet none of his characters seems really able to reconcile African and western values in a personal style. There is inevitable friction, and this may be for the good. But it means that pollution polarities touch in various places upon notions of tradition and modernity, Senegalese (or Wolof) and tubab, *African and western more generally, backward or 'bush' and civilized or evolué, and so forth. Implicated in emergent class ideologies, pollution ideas are made more complex by their linkage to globalized (or at the least Atlantic, or Franco-Senegalese) cultural differences that become internationalized under the highly extraverted form of early urbanization. Whence an expansion of the sphere of pollution to include non-modern subjects, like the beggars who take the power of their intrinsic pollution with them into the hearth of El Hadji's domestic life. Only, so the conclusion to both novella and film tells us, by admitting the abjected in all their horror to the sanctum of the family can a society begin to seek the means of making peace with itself.*

In his 'essay' Testaments Betrayed, *Milan Kundera writes of the disrespect shown the dead if those who come later do not recognize that,*

Man proceeds in the fog. But when he looks back to judge the people of the past, he sees no fog on their path. From his present, which was their faraway future, their path looks perfectly clear to him, good visibility all the way. Looking back, he sees the path, he sees the people proceeding, he sees their mistakes, but not the fog.

Xala *is thoroughly immersed in its immediate times. The film was released in Senegal, specialists tell us following Sembene's testimony, only after ten cuts had been made, mostly to do with the representation of the continuing power of France in the post-Independence period, the policy dubbed* Françafrique. *The ejection of French symbols and the delivery of attaché cases filled with notes in the overture, as well as the slightly later expulsion of the beggars led by 'Mathieu' the French head of security, were casualties of this censorship. The personality of the President of the Chamber of Commerce, his gestures and speeches, were modelled on Léopold Senghor, Senegal's first President. Several of the story's incidentals are 'factions', facts in fictional clothing, or redeployments of real circumstances: we have already noted that* Kaddu *was a predominantly Wolof-language journal supported by Sembene; the name of the chiefdom in which El Hadji's land theft occurred featured in a real land case; and the Chamber of Commerce really had been transferred to African leadership from European dominance after Independence; and Dupont-Durand had a French counterpart in Jean Collin who was a main adviser to Senghor. In these senses* Xala *is very much of the 1970s, a decade during which the lineaments of post-colonial Africa would become apparent. Sembene's antagonism to Senghor continued almost seamlessly, since he began work in 1976 on* Le dernier de L'Empire, *published in 1981 (and translated in 1983 as* The Last of Empire) *which deals with a set of characters very similar to those of* Xala, *now operating at statal level and caught up in a coup d'état against a President who has overstayed his democratic welcome. Meanwhile, Aminatu Sow Fall must have been at work writing* La grève des bàttus *(1979,* The Strike of the Begging Bowls) *a satirical account*

*of a beggars' strike in Dakar in protest at persecution by the authorities,
that feels like a reworking of Sembenesque themes and characters: not
just strikes and beggars, but bureaucratic labyrinths, unscrupulous
politicians, long-suffering wives and middle-aged men aspiring to
become polygynists.*

*Sembene drew out the feminist themes of Xala in his penultimate film,
Fat Kiine, the story of a woman who overcomes a succession of betray-
als by men: her seduction by a married school teacher which ended her
education and leaves her pregnant and alone; the rejection of herself
and her mother on account of this dishonour by her father; and her
abandonment by the conman who takes her money and leaves her
with a second pregnancy. Undaunted, the eponymous heroine cre-
ates a home for her mother, son and daughter from her income as the
proprietor of a Total petrol station in Dakar. More than just survive she
thrives, enjoying men in the way successful businessmen take lovers.
We encounter her as she drives around the Place de l'Indépendance to
drop off her daughter; women in a file cross the road ahead of her with
bright plastic bowls on their heads. And the films ends with a party on
the particularly auspicious day when she learns that her children have
passed the baccalaureate examinations that allow them entrance to
university. The two fathers appear uninvited at the celebration and are
roundly upbraided by her son who tells them their behaviour towards
his mother has forfeited the honour youth should pay to age, and children to their parents. The men and a supporter (played by the director
himself) are expelled by the guests collectively. In several respects — not
least where the films opens and how it culminates — we are invited to*

recognize variations on specific themes of Xala and a reiteration of its central critique but this time with a female lead character who by the end of the film is confidently anticipating the sexual satisfaction that eluded El Hadji.

Sembene's concerns have to a remarkable degree turned out to be those of, particularly French-language, African studies: extraversion (the turning outwards of African nation states in terms both of political economy and culture), the relation between patronage and corruption in statal politics, the appetites of the elite for consumption to excess, and just how problematic it has proved to conceive of, or achieve authentic identities. His ruggedly marxist outlook helped Sembene discern the larger shapes hiding in the fogs of the future, while his practical commitment to practising his art in Africa meant he remained attuned to everyday Senegalese realities even when they failed to match his hopes.

notes

References are to the French edition of Xala *unless the English translation is specified.*

In the interests of a more readable text, footnotes have been used to supplement the main account and our sources are acknowledged below.

first word

Pfaff (1984) and Murphy (2000) illuminate the authorship of the two versions and the circumstances of making the film. The treatment here of book and film as equally valid, complementary, narrative descriptions departs to a degree from the orthodoxy. For 'realist project' ... (Turvey 1985, Jameson 1986, also Murphy 2002 for a Brechtian comparison). *Jeune Afrique* issues from early 2013 for a sense of the Wade story in Senegalese daily newspapers at the time.

overture

Gugler (2003), a lightly expanded and updated version of Gugler and Diop (1998), is a helpful comparison of book and film. Bové (2009: 37-38) for opposition to Senghor.

From 'megalomania'... (p.9). *Il savait, comme ses pairs, se servir adroitement de ses deux pôles. La fusion n'était pas complète. (p.12). Il joua le jeu. (p.11).* Businessmen (*hommes d'affaires*).... a new kind of salesman (*commis*) (p. 105; English p. 60).

For an incisive analysis of the historical circumstances of the Senegal-ization of the Chamber of Commerce, see Boon (1992, chapter 5 'Re- appropriation of the state: the 1970s').

For vehicles, see mobilities.

patriarchy unplugged

... *moomé* or *ayé* rota (p.35). ... *pucelle* (virgin) (p.86). *Immoler* ... sacrifice (p.50; English p.27). *Salope* (p.29) ... whore (English p.13). Adesokan on decapitation (pp. 64 & 72). Fall and de Cugnac (1998) and Neveu Kringelbach (2013) for more on seduction, and its many female trappings, Senegalese style.

kleptocrats

The reduction of the Mercedes to a wooden stool is first noted in this neat way by Laura Mulvey, who has been followed by Murphy, Adesokan and others. In a footnote I suggest there is a bit more to this. In contrasting types of debt, I am grateful here to David Graeber's (2011) inspired survey. Serle et al (1977: 50) for the habits of black kites.

mobilities

On the significance of the Mercedes, see Green-Simms (2010) and Daloz (1990) for 1980s Nigeria. For SUVs (Sports Utility Vehicles), 4x4s (four-wheel drives) and Ghanaian import patterns, see Chalfin (2008), and for 'Pajero culture' in East Africa Schullenberger and Schullenberger (1998: 45). For help identifying models of Merc's, Meredith (2013).

fetishism

'Maraboutage...' freely translated from Sow (2013: 17). 'In the middle of the main room...' (English p.4) *'Au centre de la maison...'* (p. 13-14) *'le «coupé-auto-cadeau-mariage»'* (p.60) is gift-wrapped with a white ribbon just, like a 'trophy' (p.25) *'les filles et garçons d'honneur'*... are anxious to quit the parents' house to attend the reception (p.24). On poster images in Sembene's films, see Ndiaye (2010).

renown

'*Monsieur*' (p.54). Samba Gadjigo on Diéko (2010: 72-73). Gugler and Diop translate *thieli* as vulture (1998: 150). Lyric translated by Oumar Cherif Diop from the soundtrack in verse form (Gugler 2003: 135; Gugler and Diop 1998: 152-3). On caste, see Diagne (2004: 248, 256-63); the issue is raised more explicitly in Sembene's *Le Dernier de l'empire*; on the real-life referents of *Kaddu*, see Diagne (2004: 182, n7).

soundscapes

Comparsita... le Jerk... la Pachanga (p. 46). Having been party to the general misconception, also shared by web-based sources, I owe correction of the identification of the vocalist of *Etoiles de Dakar* to Gérald Arnaud (2008). For a Wolof version of the beggar's song, see Adesokan (2011: 63).

denouement

... *matières fécales.* (p.185). damp and pungent (p. 105, English p. 60). Mercedes ... Serigne Mada (p.134-5). '*la benne des éboueux passaient*', 'the rubbish carts passed by' (p. 161, English p. 94), '*La benne des éboueux collectait des ordures du matin, faisant escale devant chaque maison*' (p.178). '*Ce qu'une main a planté, une autre peut ôter*' (p. 51). The description of the salubrious character of this road is repeated (p.178). Harrow argues that the moment in the lift equates to El Hadji's fall (2004: 130). Conclusions to the novella are quoted from the English (p. 113) and French (p. 190); the double blank space before the final sentence is in both versions.

last word

On caste among Mande, see Conrad and Frank (1996). SET and SETAL, see Roberts and Nooter Roberts (2003: 135-7), Diouf (1992, 1996), Harney (2004: 205-16). Youssou N'Dour's album *Set* with English translation of lyrics was released internationally by Virgin in 1990. Milan Kundera (1995: 240).

talking heads

p. 28 being all for modernity does not mean losing our africanity adapted from '*Si nous sommes pour la modernité, cela ne veut pas dire que nous avons renoncé à notre Africanité*', the President of the Chamber of Commerce (*Xala* p. 9)

p. 47 you have to prepare the ground (i.e. for sowing) '*Il faut labourer son champ*', (literally, 'you have to plough your field') Mama Fatou, N'Goné's mother, reproaching her husband, Babacar, for leaving their daughter's marriage prospects to God and fortune (*Xala* p.16).

p. 59 a ruler should not behave like the lizard adapted from Oumar Cherif Diouf's translation of Ousmane Sembene's lyric for the beggars' song, see p. 100-1 here.

p. 66 everybody will have their turn from Oumar Cherif Diouf's translation of Ousmane Sembene's lyric for the beggars' song, see p. 101 here.

p. 82 what one hand has planted, another can pull up '*Ce qu'une main a planté, une autre peut l'ôter*', addressed to El Hadji about his *xala* by the woman who carried the cockerel to be killed should there be no blood of deflowering on the wedding night, *Xala* p. 51; for the converse of this, see Serigne Mada recounting his own reported speech to El Hadji who has not recognized him, '*Ce qu'il a enlevé, il peut le replanter*', 'What he has lifted, he can replant', *Xala* p. 166.

p. 93 the lion will not be denied his desire for want of courage adapted from Oumar Cherif Diouf's translation of Ousmane Sembene's lyric for the beggars' song, see p. 101 here.

p. 102 for everything there is a season from Oumar Cherif Diouf's translation of Ousmane Sembene's lyric for the beggars' song, see p. 101 here.

p. 121 instead of crying, you have to find a solution for your problems from Oumar Cherif Diouf's translation of Ousmane Sembene's lyric for the beggars' song, see p. 101 here.

references

Adesokan, Akin 2011 *Postcolonial Artists and Global Aesthetics*, Bloomington: Indiana University Press.

Arnaud, Gérald 2008 *Youssou N'Dour: le griot planétaire*, Paris: Voix du Monde, Éditions Demi-Lune.

Boone, Catherine 1992 *Merchant Capital and the Roots of State Power in Senegal: 1930-1985*, Cambridge Studies in Comparative Politics, Cambridge University Press.

Bové, Bruno 2009 'Sembène Ousmane (1923-2007), une biographie', in Diat and Barlet, pp. 26-45.

Busch, Annett and Max Annas 2008 *Ousmane Sembène – Interviews*, Jackson: University Press of Mississippi.

Chalfin, Brenda 2008 'Cars, the Custom Service, and sumptuary rule in neoliberal Ghana', *Comparative Studies in Society and Culture* 50(2): 424-53.

Conrad, David C. and Barbara E. Frank (eds) 1995 *Status and Identity in West Africa: Nyamakalaw of Mande*, Bloomington: Indiana University Press.

Daloz, Jean-Pascal (1990) 'Voitures et prestige au Nigeria', *Politique Africaine* June 38: 148-53.

Dia, Thieno Ibrahima and Olivier Barlet (eds) 2009 *Sembène Ousmane (1923-2007), Africultures* (76), Paris: L'Harmattan.

Diagne, Ismaïla 2004 *Les Sociétés africaines au miroir de Sembène Ousmane*, Paris: Karthala.

Diouf, Jean-Léopold 2003 *Dictionnaire wolof-français et français-wolof*, Paris: Karthala.

Diouf, Mamadou 1992 'Fresques murales et écriture de l'histoire. Le *Set/Setal* à Dakar', *Politique Africaine* 46: 41-54.

Diouf, Mamadou 1996 'Urban youth and Senegalese politics: Dakar 1988-1994', *Public Culture* 8: 225-49.

Fall, Sokhna and Fabien de Cugnac 1998 *Séduction: cinq leçons sénégalaises*, Paris: Editions Alternatives.

Fanon, Frantz 1952 *Peau noire, masques blancs*, Paris: Seuil.

Fofana, Amadou T. 2012 *The Films of Ousmane Sembène: discourse, politics, and culture*, Amherst: Cambria Press.

Gadjigo, Samba 2010 (originally 2007) *Ousmane Sembène: the making of a militant artist*, translated by Moustapha Diop, Bloomington and Indianapolis: Indiana University Press.

Graeber, David 2011 *Debt: the first 5,000 years*, Brooklyn New York: Melville House.

Green-Simms, Lindsey 2010 'The return of the Mercedes: from Ousmane Sembene to Kenneth Nnebue', in Mahir Saul and Ralph A. Austen (eds) *Viewing African Cinema in the Twenty-First Century: art films and the Nollywood video revolution*, Ohio UP.

Gugler, Josef and Oumar Cherif Diop 1998 'Ousmane Sembène's "Xala": the novel, the film, and their audiences', *Research in African Literatures* 29(2): 147-158.

Gugler, Josef 2003 'Xala 1974 – impotence sexual, cultural, economic, and political', in his *African Film: Re-imagining a Continent*, James Currey, pp. 126-38.

Harney, Elizabeth 2004 *In Senghor's Shadow: art, politics, and the avant-garde in Senegal 1960-1995*, Durham and London: Duke University Press.

Harrow, Kenneth W. 2004 'The failed trickster', in Pfaff pp. 124-42.

Jameson, Fredric 1986 'Third World literature in the era of multinational capitalism', *Social Text* 15: 65-88.

Kundera, Milan 1995 (originally 1993) *Testaments Betrayed: an essay in nine parts*, translated by Linda Asher, London: Faber and Faber.

Meredith, Laurence 2003 *Mercedes-Benz Saloons. The classic models of the 1960s and 1970s*, Wiltshire: Crowood Press.

Mulvey, Laura. 1991 'Xala, Ousamane Sembene 1976, the carapace that failed' *Third Text* 16/17: 19-37.

Murphy, David 2000 'The indiscreet charm of the African bourgeoisie? Consumerism, fetishism & socialism in *Xala*', Chapter 4 of his *Sembene: imagining alternatives in film and fiction*, Oxford: James Currey.

Murphy, David 2002 'An African Brecht. The cinema of Ousmane Sembene', *New Left Review* 16 (July-August): 115-29.

Ndiaye, Hadja Maï Niang 2010 'Les autres arts de Sembène Ousmane entre l'écrit et l'écran: les photos et les portraits peints de révolutionnaires', in Samba Gadjigo and Sada Niang (eds) *Un viatique pour l'éternité. Hommage à Ousmane Sembène*, Dakar: Editions Papyrus Afrique, pp. 107-19.

Neveu Kringelbach, Hélène 2013 *Dance Circles: movement, morality and self-fashioning in urban Senegal*, Oxford: Berghahn.

Niang, Sada 2012 'Neorealism and nationalist African cinemas', in Soverio Giovacchini and Robert Sklar (eds) *Global Neorealism: the transnational history of a film style*, Jackson: University of Mississippi, pp. 194-208.

Petty, Sheila 2010 'Pugnacité et pouvoir: le representation des femmes dans les films d'Ousmane Sembène', in Samba Gadjigo and Sada Niang (eds) *Un viatique pour l'éternité. Hommage à Ousmane Sembène*, Dakar: Editions Papyrus Afrique, pp. 17-52.

Pfaff, Françoise 1984 *The Cinema of Ousmane Sembene, a pioneer of African film*, Westport Conn. and London: Contributions in Afro-American and African Studies, Number 79, Greenwood Press.

Pfaff, Françoise (ed.) 2004 *Focus on African Films*, Bloomington: Indiana University Press.

Roberts, Allen F. and Mary Nooter Roberts 2003 *A Saint in the City: sufi arts of urban Senegal*, Los Angeles: UCLA Fowler Museum.

Schullenberger, Bonnie and William Schullenberger 1998 *Africa Time: two scholars' seasons in Uganda*, Lanham: University Press of America.

Sembène, Ousmane 1966 *Vehi-Ciosane ou Blanche-Genèse suivi du Mandat*, Paris and Dakar: Présence Africaine.

Sembène, Ousmane 1973 *Xala*, Dakar and Paris: Présence Africaine.

Sembene, Ousmane 1976 *Xala*, translated by Clive Wake, London, Nairobi, Ibadan: Heineman African Writers Series.

Sembene, Ousmane 1983 (originally 1981) *The Last of Empire. A Senegalese novel*, translated by Adrian Adams, London, Nairobi, Ibadan: Heineman African Writers Series.

Sembène, Ousmane 1996 *Guelwaar*, Paris and Dakar: Présence Africaine.

Serle, W, G.J. Morel and W. Hartig 1977 *A Field Guide to the Birds of West Africa*, Glasgow: William Collins.

Sow, Ibrahima 2013 *Le Maraboutage au Sénégal*, Dakar: IFAN Ch. A. Diop.

Sow-Fall, Aminata 1979 *La Grève des bàttu, ou, Les Déchets humains*, Collection Motifs No 124.

Sow-Fall, Aminata 1981 *The Beggars' Strike, or, The Dregs of Society*, translated by Dorothy S. Blair, Harlow: Longman.

Turvey, Gerry 1985 '"Xala" and the curse of neo-colonialism. Reflections on a realist project', *Screen* 26(3/4): 75-87.

acknowledgements

Paul Gifford and Yumiko Yokozeki for the warmth of their, repeated, hospitality in Dakar and their practical encouragement, not least Paul's detailed comments on two drafts; Gabriel Klaeger for conversation about transportation; the University of Edinburgh for the invitation to deliver some elements of this account as an annual lecture in the series dedicated to the memory of the much-missed Charles Jedrej, and for helpful comments on that occasion.

Printed in 2017
in India